Striking a dramatic pose, Mr Muriel (left) and Mr Veness (right) celebrating their joint 'Birthday Extravaganza', some years ago.

About the Authors

David Muriel was born in Islington, London, in 1943. He first studied at Hastings School of Art and then went on to train at Beckenham School of Art and Ravensbourne College of Art and Design, where he studied graphic design. Having worked for several designers and architects in both this country and abroad, he eventually decided to run his own design practice until pursuing a teaching career in education, finally retiring to his family home in Kent.

Bruce Veness was born in Hastings, Sussex, in 1943. He studied at Hastings School of Art and Goldsmiths College, London. As well as his development as an artist, he has had a lifelong involvement in the theatre, acting, designing, and directing. When he met his actress wife Jill, they started their own theatre company where they produced both classical and contemporary dramas. Bruce has also taught art and coached students for drama school. Both he and Jill now live in rural France with their animals.

This, however, is the writers' first attempt at co-writing a book.

Illustrations by Bruce Veness

GRIDLOCK SPUMES
AND
'THE CASE WITH NO NAME'

A fictional spine-tingling adventure, not for the faint-hearted

David Muriel and Bruce Veness

GRIDLOCK SPUMES
AND
'THE CASE WITH NO NAME'

Olympia Publishers
London

www.olympiapublishers.com
OLYMPIA PAPERBACK EDITION

A CIP catalogue record for this title is
available from the British Library.

ISBN: 978-1-84897-447-0

(Olympia Publishers is part of Ashwell Publishing Ltd)

This is a work of fiction.
Names, characters, places and incidents originate from the writers'
imagination. Any resemblance to actual persons, living or dead,
is purely coincidental.

First Published in 2014

Olympia Publishers
60 Cannon Street
London
EC4N 6NP

Printed in Great Britain

Acknowledgements

Mr Muriel would like to thank his cousin Penny for her literary expertise and her sons, Adam and Greg, for their guidance and help with the complexities of computer technology.

Mr Veness would like to express his gratitude to his wife Jill, for her ongoing patience and perseverance in the production of the manuscript.

We would also like to thank the dedicated friends who painstakingly read through the text giving feedback advice (some of which is unprintable).

Warning to readers with a nervous disposition:

This book contains occasional references to flatulence, cross-dressing and liquorice allsorts.

Contents

About this book

This tragic tale begins in London in the late 1800s, in which our hero, ace detective Gridlock Spumes, (misguided by his own self-importance) agrees to help the plight of a beautiful woman who is being blackmailed. She accompanies him, along with his manservant, to a sanatorium in deepest rural France, where foul play is suspected. Plot and counter plot is uncovered resulting in them returning to England, where play is even fouler, as the country's prize treasures have been stolen, masterminded by the detective's arch enemy. The case finally leads our intrepid group into the capital's dark and dangerous criminal underworld where they witness the deceit and corruption of high-ranking officials.

Foreword

Long, long ago in a Twitterless, Facebook, Wikipedia, iPod, iPhone, Playstation, texting, and emailing-free world, two young art students met and discovered that along with most of their contemporaries they shared an identical, off-beat, surreal and lunatic sense of humour. In other words they were hopelessly devoted to their hero, the late comic genius Spike Milligan* (he was always late) and his groundbreaking radio series *The Goon Show*. Bruce Veness, who now lives in deepest France and David Muriel who lives in deepest Kent have remained friends and during their occasional meetings continue to converse in the imbecile language and voices of Eccles, Bluebottle, Moriarty,

---

*Mr Muriel recalls meeting Spike with some trepidation, quite by chance, at a book signing in Rye, Sussex, during the late 1990s: I mentioned to him that while reading his book *Puckoon* on a train journey, it had reduced me to hysterics (much to the dismay of the other passengers). This novel, he considered was undoubtedly his best written work. He asked if I lived locally.

"No, Hastings," I answered, "You get a better class of criminal there," I joked.

He chuckled and signed my book. We talked further about his poetry, but realising that I was now holding up a queue of fans that had formed behind me to have their books signed, he whispered, "Now bugger off."

My response was, "Isn't that illegal?"

"Well fuck off then," he said grinning and with that, I took his advice.

Bloodknock, Grytpype-Thynne, Neddy and the Cruns. Sad isn't it?

After several glasses of red wine had been sunk at one of their rare reunions, it was suggested that they should attempt to co-write a spoof on Sherlock Holmes as a kind of tribute to Spike. Six or seven glasses later, Mr Veness offered to start the ball rolling and he duly produced the first instalment of the saga, which was emailed to Mr Muriel back in 'Old Blighty'. He in turn read it and wished he'd never agreed to such a crazy project. However, he rose to the challenge and duly continued the story where his co-author had left off, and emailed back the next instalment. And so it continued, both writers picking up where the other had left off and neither of them knowing what the hell was coming next. After months of communications flying to and fro across the Channel, the story finally reached its inevitable conclusion. The authors sincerely hope that you, the reader, can make more sense of it than they are able to.

This captivating little tale was written and compiled under pressure due to extreme boredom. Most of the characters, some places and all of the events mentioned are strictly fictional to protect the guilty. Factual discrepancies throughout have been purposefully written in to enhance the story, and to save the authors the insurmountable task of double-checking. In the unlikely event of readers finding mistakes of any kind, we ask you to please keep it to yourselves and don't ring us.

Chapter 1

Lady Puke confesses all

Gridlock Spumes sank back contentedly into his well-worn leather armchair, crossed his eyes, legs and fingers, and stared pensively through the window at the yellow fog, which swirled against the glass panes on the gas-lit world outside. It was dusk, time for his customary smoke and time to contemplate a strange case that had recently caught his attention. It was a small brown Gladstone that had been left on his doorstep, which on inspection revealed a strange collection of unrelated objects. Inside the leather bag was a well worn Yupik Eskimo Mukluk boot (left foot only), its sole constructed of a nauseous-smelling arctic seal's flipper; a pawn ticket for a set of wooden dentures, from Jobaz Wilson of Coburg Square; a jar of Dr Scrotum's pile ointment, available from most reputable chemists; and finally, a selection of ladies' silk undergarments, which on nasal inspection were strongly musk-scented. *Very interesting*, he thought. Among these strange items was an embarkation slip for the Cunard passenger ship *The Ruritania,* due to depart from Southampton the following afternoon. On the back of this was a somewhat rude cryptic handwritten message addressed to 'H' that read: 'Solve this one you clever bastard' and signed 'M'. Baffled, he made a note to remind his manservant to take the bag to Scotland Yard Forensic Department, to have it thoroughly forensic'd.

This whole episode however has nothing whatsoever to do with our story, but it does give you, the reader, some insight into the perceptiveness and razor-sharp working mind of our detective, when confronted with cunning criminal resourcefulness at this early stage of the proceedings. Vacantly, he filled and lit his reproduction Japanese papier-mâché meerschaum, and drew upon it deeply. However, illustration was not his strongest attribute. In an instant the bowl of the pipe was in flames, and instinctively, he grabbed for the soda siphon next to him and directed the nozzle at the flaming pipe, still clenched between his teeth. He squeezed the trigger and a steady stream of liquid drenched both the flaming meerschaum and Spumes himself. Slowly, and with as much dignity as he could muster, he removed his cardboard string-tasselled smoking cap, and wiped the wet soot from his blackened face. Muttering vile oaths he began to tear the sodden article into small pieces which he rolled, and then flicked deliberately in the direction of Doctor Phuckwytte Prunestone, his manservant, and regular erstwhile companion. Prunestone, who was perfecting his pirouettes at the time, jumped upon the couch excitedly and began to catch the projectiles in his bowler hat, which he held high.

He then shouted, "God bless the Queen! Hoorah for Gridlock!" and at the same instant he leapt balletically from the couch, performing a pas-de-deux around the room proudly adorned in his new sackcloth tutu and matching seaweed hairpiece.

"Enough," cried Gridlock who rose to half his height and hopped backwards towards the now red-faced and perspiring doctor. "Now Prunestone, I wish to play something to sooth my nerves," he commanded. Prunestone, eager to please, rummaged through the antique chest of drawers and returned with a pack of cards, which he offered to his master.

"Fool," cried Gridlock giving Phuckwytte one of his withering looks, which he handed back immediately. "I meant the violin," the detective answered, as he flicked open its battered case from which he took the instrument, placed it between his knees, the bow between his teeth and his teeth between his fingers. He then began to play passionately, Ivanitch Immicrutchki's melancholic 'Lug Wormers Lament' in D flat major minus F sharp removed. After this melodic performance, Gridlock carefully replaced the Stradivarius back in its case, as the final note lingered on and slowly drifted away through the open door, into the lavatory, out through the open window and down into the foggy street below, where it found its way to the little Fish & Chip Emporium on the corner.

Prunestone, tears streaming down his silk tights and into his waders, sobbed, "Only you could play such a demanding piece without strings."

"Nonsense," replied the Gridlock puffing away at his pipe. "I know of at least one man who could play that piece, almost as well as myself, with his eyes closed and his hands tied behind his back."

"Who?" enquired the doctor in disbelief?

"Genghis Phart, that cross-eyed Albanian chicken-sexer, the right hand and occasionally left foot of my arch enemy, the evil genius Doctor Gonad Varicosi PhD (failed) – may he rot in hell."

Gridlock then began to shake violently, threw himself to the floor where he gyrated grotesquely, foaming at the mouth.

"Allsorts," he cried, clutching at his throat.

"What, man?" shouted the panic-stricken doctor.

"Fetch my allsorts!" croaked Gridlock. "A quarter of a pound, I need them now."

Knowing of Spume's compulsive desire for the vile substance, Prunestone fetched the lead-lined wooden tea caddy from the mantelpiece, which contained the only drug that could now satisfy the sleuth's mad craving. His journey of addiction had commenced with an innocent bag of sherbet lemons, which eventually led him to his uncontrollable addiction to the hard-line liquorice allsorts, which he now stuffed feverishly into his mouth, nose and ears. Swallowing the last morsel, Spumes attempted to compose himself, got up and stood on one leg and faced the wall, something he always did when he felt ashamed or guilt-ridden.

"Prunestone," coughed the detective. "It's time for you to get out of those working clothes and dress for dinner, which if I'm not mistaken, will be served at eight o'clock sharp in the dining room. We have much to discuss." With this, the doctor pirouetted from the room, and collided with the jardinière, which sent the aspidistra flying.

Later that evening as the dinner gong sounded, Gridlock strode elegantly into the kerosene-lit dining room, resplendent in his heavily embroidered, purple quilted, smoking jacket; a new cerise cotton-rich smoking hat; and his great uncle's string smoking-kilt proudly woven into the family tartan of McSpumes. A removable duelling scar down his right cheek completed the ensemble. Spumes caught his reflection in the mirror, let out a cry of anguish, threw the false facial addition into the spittoon, and sat down at the table, toying with his eye patch – something he wore when he was about to embark upon a new case.

Phuckwytte entered and seated himself opposite his master. He was wearing a whalebone corset beneath a low-cut black silk ball gown, that was adorned with his mother's best paste jewellery. His hair was up and arranged carefully under his tiara. Even though it was his only hair, it had been brushed and styled to perfection. Stroking his ginger sideburns and moustache, he inhaled deeply from the cigar he was smoking, coughed violently and asked, "What's up old chap, why the rum boat race?"

Gridlock raised his head slowly, stared at his companion and replied, "God man, you look ridiculous. If I've told you once, I've told you a hundred times, that black silk does not complement your complexion." Phuckwytte, visibly hurt, looked down at the florid oilskin tablecloth and whispered that he would only wear the plum velvet in future.

"Now to business," said the detective, pouring a rich dark Vimto Grand Cru 69 into the crystal wine glasses. "I have received a letter from a Lady Bulimia Puke imploring us to help her. Apparently she is being blackmailed by a person or persons unknown, for exceedingly large sums of money, and the poor creature is beside herself with anxiety and fear."

"About what, may I ask?" enquired Phuckwytte.

"Aaahh," replied Gridlock raising his eyebrows, lowering them and then wiggling them from left to right. "Prepare yourself Prunestone, for what I am about to unfold to you is a most shocking and unsettling story of a crime, so horrible, that even I myself have been profoundly disturbed by its revelation."

As the wind howled outside and the lamps began to flicker, the noise of unearthly creakings and groanings were followed by a slow thump... thump... thump... Gridlock at once recognised the familiar sound of Lilly Haemorrhoid's wooden peg leg. Lilly had been 'in service' with the detective for the past thirteen years as his live-in cook and housekeeper. The door slowly opened, and she stood there holding a steaming tray of food that she had destroyed in her own inimitable way. She was not amused and began to hurl knives, forks, spoons and other accoutrements into a pile upon the table, as she muttered sullenly about dinner always being served at eight-thirty and no sooner.

"Not that it matters anyway, because there's some hoity-toity woman by the name of Lady Puke to see you downstairs. And I cooked your favourite too, crapeau dans le trou (toad in the hole), avec puree de pommes de terre (mashed spuds) and for dessert, Richard avec les zits et la crème anglaise (spotted dick and custard)." The words were hardly out of her mouth before the pair had barged past, propelling her and her tray of culinary delights along the landing. The two men mounted the stair rail and careered down the staircase at a frightening speed.

They landed as one onto the ground floor hallway where there stood the attractive, and impeccably dressed, Lady Bulimia Puke. She eyed Gridlock approvingly, as he attempted to extricate himself from his floundering manservant. Rising steadily, pulling down his kilt, which was now over his head, he rearranged his feather sporran, adjusted his smoking hat and eye patch, and bowed gracefully.

"Lady Puke, I presume. Allow me to introduce myself. I am Gridlock Spumes, and this is my friend Doctor Phuckwytte Prunestone." The unfortunate Phuckwytte struggled to his feet, curtsied, and self-consciously rearranged his tiara.

"Delighted to meet you Madam," he muttered.

"Charmed," she responded.

"Come let us retire to the drawing room," said Gridlock leading the way. Their visitor arranged herself on the leather couch, while her host stood in front of the blazing fire raising his kilt to warm his backside. The doctor, on the other hand, ensconced himself in an armchair and toyed with his jewellery.

"Now, how may I be of assistance?" enquired Gridlock. "Please speak freely, Madame. Prunestone here is a complete cretin of the first order and will not understand any words you may convey."

"I wreally don't know where to begin," she replied, letting out a little sob and dabbing her cheeks delicately with one of her husband's old socks.

"It is a long sad stowry which began while Lord Methane Puke and I were honeymooning in Fwrance," she continued. "We had spent a wonderful day picnicking in the Cwruese Valley, a delightfully wrural area inhabited by illitewrate, inbwred and gwrowth-stunted half-wits. Our coachman chanced upon a charming Inn called 'The Auberge De Gwranchez' and we were delighted to discover that the propwrietors, a Monsieur Weginald and Madame Ethel Spiggott, were English. This couple also wran an adjoining Sanatowrium where they cared for severely and mentally challenged ex-patwriots."

"Wait a moment," interrupted Gridlock. "You can't be too careful. Prunestone, the curtains."

"Yes, they are lovely aren't they?" observed Phuckwytte.

"Draw them immediately," ordered Gridlock, and Phuckwytte obediently danced to the drawer of an antique leather-topped Jacobean writing desk, brought out an antique, leather-topped Jacobean pencil and parchment, and hummed tunelessly whilst he sketched.

Gridlock's posterior was now being severely scorched and had taken on the appearance of corned beef. He moved carefully, re-arranged his kilt and sat next to Bulimia.

"Pray continue, Lady Puke," he encouraged, his voice now approaching castrato as the hairs on his scrotum were caught between the buttons of the leather chesterfield. "But please madam, lower your voice, since we may be overheard."

"Well, as I was saying," she continued, in a deep masculine baritone. "Methane and I thought we might take shelter for the night since my husband, twrue to his name, needed to wretire, this being attwributed to a call of nature and some urgency was wrequired to wresolve the situation. Flatulence can be such a pwroblem on a long journey don't you find?" she explained.

"It's not exactly beneficial on a short journey madam," admitted the detective. The unfortunate memory of the affair caused the lady to burst into an uncontrollable outburst of tears, the black dye from her husband's old sock smudged her face, and this, combined with her lowered voice now gave Gridlock the impression of Paul Robeson in the film *Sanders of the River* (yet to be made in 1935). They all stood up and sang the words:

"'Ol' Man River'," and promptly sat down again.

"Carry on Bulimia; I can call you Bulimia can't I?" Gridlock asked.

"You just did," she replied and continued, "We were intwroduced to the owners of this delightful hostel, Madame and Monsieur Spiggott, both English by birth, Welsh by nature and Irish by consent." At this point Bulimia blew her nose loudly.

"Farrah!" causing the sock to disintegrate.

"This charming couple were both late in their years and as it happened, late with everything else apart from our bill," she complained.

"I see," muttered Gridlock, as he lovingly patted the head of his mangy, stuffed guard dog, Ringworm, causing it to release a cloud of sawdust.

"So do I!" exclaimed Phuckwytte leaping forward, parchment in hand. "There!" he proudly announced, showing them the drawing he had painstakingly made of the curtains and pelmet. Gridlock glared at him through his monocle, snatched the inept scribble and inspected it.

"Not one of your finest renderings Prunestone," said his master, throwing the treasured piece back in the artist's face.

"I'm doing my best," whined Phuckwytte.

"Your best is not good enough," he retorted and with that criticism Phuckwytte turned and flounced from the room, stepping into the half filled brass spittoon, dragging it with him.

"He seems such a sensitive little woman," remarked Bulimia.

"Pay no heed, he's just an attention seeker," said Gridlock. "Would you care for some liquid refreshment my dear?" he asked.

"That would be wonderful!" she beamed. Gridlock went over to the window and pulled on the servants' bell cord, which promptly broke and fell to the floor to the sound of a toilet flushing. Returning, he sat next to his guest once more.

"My dear lady, please continue," he cooed, for despite her now blackened face and baritone voice he felt drawn to her, moving closer, intoxicated by her sweet, heady perfume. Risqué thoughts filtered through his mind as he gazed into her large tearful eyes.

She stared up at him and enquired, "What's that up your nose?" Gridlock sneezed and a liquorice allsort shot past her left ear, ricocheting off the mantelpiece.

"Sorry," he said self-consciously.

"That's quite alwright," she replied wiping her face with the back of her hand. "I quite like the taste of liquowrice."

Gridlock, much to his alarm, noticed that his sporran had taken on a life of its own, and had begun to move of its own accord. Trying to control his pent up emotions, he rested his hands upon his lap and listened intently to her unfortunate tale.

Apparently, the Spiggotts had been most accommodating to the couple; they were offered the honeymoon suite, which was part of a converted barn which adjoined the Sanatorium and overlooked the highly-fenced exercise yard where patients with more severe mental problems were allowed some freedom. The overall impression was that despite its charming exterior, the property and its owners had fallen on hard times, since the sanitary arrangements for guests under the stairs consisted of simply a galvanized bucket, a damp sponge and a copy of *The Creuse Farming Gazette,* which had been torn into strips and folded to a point. An attempt to signify affluence no doubt, though not a very absorbent solution, but typically French.

"We were woken in the night by an awful scwreem," she sobbed. "Methane went to inwestigate weawring his silk stwriped nightshirt and cap." She broke down again at the memory.

"It was dwreadful," she wailed.

"I don't know, a silk striped nightshirt and cap can be quite fetching," remarked Gridlock, as he slid his arm around her comfortingly. "There, there, my dear, please don't take it so hard."

"How else do you expect me to take it?" she cried. He was about to reply, but was interrupted by a thumping noise outside which became progressively louder. Lilly had returned and was now standing in the doorway, her hair in curling rags, and with a lit cigarette hanging from her mouth. She was attired in a stained apron and a woollen stocking, which was rolled down to her remaining ankle, revealing a varicose-veined leg, looking not unlike the tributary system of the Nile. A greasy food-splattered skirt completed her outfit.

"You rang luv?" she moaned, as she stood brazenly with her arms folded.

"Tea, Lilly," ordered Gridlock.

"I'd love some duck," she retorted, taking a long drag on her fag end and blowing a smoke ring into the air.

"No, could you please bring us some," he commanded angrily.

"But you ain't yet eaten that lovely nosh I cooked for yer," she croaked.

"Lilly!" shouted Gridlock, and she acquiesced begrudgingly with the choice of, "Dandelion, Darjeelin' or that Lapsang muck you always 'ave?"

"The Lapsang muck," Gridlock sighed.

"Suppose you'll want the best bone china then," she enquired, looking at Bulimia.

"Please," he said. And with that she attempted to curtsey, but her unfortunate disability made it practically impossible, so turning on her wooden leg (making yet another hole in the threadbare carpet) she exited in a huff, slamming the door behind her.

"You just can't get the staff these days," Gridlock complained.

"I know exactly what you mean, Mr Spumes," Bulimia responded.

"Call me Gridlock," he murmured.

"We were forced to dismiss Chilvers, one of our gwroundsmen, for mounting one of our garden statues on the west tewrrace," she exclaimed.

"Erecting a garden statue isn't a sackable offence, surely?"

"No, but sexual molestation is," she whispered as her cheeks coloured. "And in bwroad daylight too. The shame of it," she uttered.

"Heavens," said Gridlock, not knowing what to say.

"Dwrunk of course, he'd been pilfering daddy's best bwrandy from the cellar," she continued.

"Gosh, how extremely embarrassing for you," he agreed.

Lady Bulimia Puke had come from good, upper class stock; the family name Bentley (like the future car to be built in 1921) was strong, solid and built to last. Her father, Lord Bullstrode Bentley, was the MP for West Wittering, Selsey, and her mother, Lady Wilhelmina Bentley, was involved in charity work for the poor. Bulimia had wanted for nothing; her future had already been decided and mapped out for her. Finishing school in Switzerland and her 'coming out' had both been recorded in *The Tatler*. Among the fortunate few from the privileged classes who were destined to achieve, she had first met Methane Puke at a polo match where he had been accidentally knocked out cold with a mallet. With his front teeth missing, nose broken and his black eyes crossed, it was love at first sight and whilst cradling him in her arms, the sight of blood had prompted her to vomit. From then on it was a whirlwind romance, and they were married in the private chapel on her parents' estate.

According to her, the honeymoon in France had not been her choice, but her husband's suggestion in order to economise.

"He is a tight-fisted aristocwrat," she confided. Also, he hadn't been much help during the whole unfortunate affair. On the contrary, he'd been quite hopeless, and that is why she now had to seek professional assistance. Gridlock rose, while still listening, and went over to the large ornate fish tank displayed on the oak cabriole-legged sideboard and playfully tapped on the glass, disturbing Sputum, his pet Portuguese man-of-war jellyfish, which promptly ascended in globular fashion to the surface, only to dive to the bottom of the tank and hide under some coral.

"Tell me, this scream at the Auberge… what colour was it?" he asked.

"It was difficult to tell because I had my back to it and poor Methane is colour-blind," she confessed.

"Hmm…" Gridlock stroked his chin thoughtfully. This case had now caught his interest.

"Notice anything else unusual?" he asked. She thought for a moment.

"We overheard a piano being played in the main house, the opening part of Gwrieg's Piano Concerto in A Minor, which stopped abwruptly and was followed by a loud sneeze," she remembered.

"Do go on," he prompted.

She looked embarrassed again and continued, "The chamber pot under the bed had alwready been soiled, along with the sink and the elephant's foot wastepaper basket!"

"The bounder must have been on the run!" Gridlock exclaimed.

"Evidently," she replied. "I also found a wrecently stubbed out Havana cigar in the ashtwray on my bedside table, and a pickled hewrring under my pillow."

So he was now looking for a three-legged incontinent elephant with a cold, that smoked cigars, and loved playing classical music on the piano. But who had screamed, and where the pickled herring came into the picture? He had no idea. Fantasy and reality now became blurred. He now knew that his investigations would have to take place in France.

She handed him an envelope saying, "This came thwrough my letter box this morning." He opened it to reveal a circus programme that advertised 'The Great Castrato', hypnotist, illusionist, mind reader and part-time scrap metal dealer'. On the reverse side was handwritten: 'Rap 5 tousent lira roun' a smok't kippr an' leaf in'a ladis lavs at Savoy ho tell'.

"Bloody illiterate swine," snarled Gridlock and admitted, "Confusing, isn't it, dear reader?" and returned to the plot.

Meanwhile, the door opened, and Phuckwytte made a grand entrance, resplendent in an enormous coiffed ginger wig, full make-up, fake lapis lazuli earrings, crimson-sequinned ball gown with matching handbag and gloves, a white feather boa and bright yellow fisherman's waders.

"I'm just off to the shops," he gaily announced.

"You're a little overdwressed aren't you?" observed Bulimia.

"You never know who you'll meet at the cheese counter," came the response.

"The fisherman's waders clash a bit don't they?" remarked Gridlock.

"It's raining and I might get drenched."

"Arrested more like," his master joked.

Undeterred, Phuckwytte enquired, "Anything you need?"

"Get me two ounces of Black Shag from Bradley's in Oxford Street. Oh, and go to Fortnum's for some caviar, a bottle of Vintage Grand Cru Vimto, the special honey and balsam for my bath, and put the lot on my account."

"But you haven't got an account," bleated Phuckwytte.

"Don't argue man, do it! And while you're there, collect my Harris Tweed hunting jacket and breeches from the Sunlight, the ticket is on the bureau."

"Going hunting?" Bulimia asked.

"No I just love the material," he confessed. Now, looking into her sweet face he asked, "I'll need your assistance if I am to resolve this case. Could you possibly come with us to France, or do you think your husband would object?"

"On the contwrary, it's the 'poaching season' and he's busy helping my father shooting on the estate," she explained.

"Pheasant?" enquired Gridlock.

"No, poachers," she conceded.

"That's settled then, we've no time to lose. Prunestone!" he said handing him some petty cash. "Book first-class seats for this lady and myself on the Continental Express from Victoria Station to Dover, and two first-class cabins on the ferry to Calais."

"What about me?" Phuckwytte asked.

"You, my dear doctor, will be travelling third class and looking after the luggage as usual."

"But I always travel third class."

"Don't argue, just get on with it!" ordered Gridlock. With that Phuckwytte threw the feather boa over his shoulder and did an about turn, (his wig remaining in the same position) and minced out of the room.

Cross-dressing had been a way of life for him, ever since he had tried on his mother's brassiere when he was but twelve years old, and was enamoured by the reflection in her dressing table mirror. It had been a strange adventure ever since: a disciplinary hearing concerning the wearing of girls' knickers and lipstick in the gym had led to his expulsion from school. Dressing in an evening gown with pearls and flamboyant ostrich feathered hat at his passing out parade at Sandhurst did not further his military career either. After his discharge he worked as a part-time usherette at the Strand Palace Theatre. Alas, he was given notice, however, when a member of the audience spotted his walrus moustache and sideburns as he entered the ladies' convenience during a lengthy recital performance of music hall singer Nelly Bowels, which resulted in his position being immediately terminated. During his candid transvestite 'career' he'd had many short acquaintances, mostly with height challenged gentlemen, and had been a great favourite with the sailors on shore leave and with dockers in the Pool of London. But it was not only his attempt at cross-dressing that proved to be a failure, for his title of Medical Doctor was as false as his bogus sexuality. Gridlock had found him wandering the streets half starved and had taken pity on him, taking him in as his valet, diplomatically turning a blind eye to his quirky fetish for wearing feminine attire. Phuckwytte was nevertheless determined to show his worth and perhaps this new case would give him the opportunity. Anyway, because his master wore an eye patch, in his opinion, he assumed that three eyes were better than one.

Clasping the laundry ticket, he gracefully descended the stone steps onto the wet pavement of a bustling Baker Street, with its jostle of umbrellas, and hailed a hansom cab.

"Where to madam?" enquired the driver.

"Victoria Station and don't spare the horse," he ordered and sat back considering what their next move would be. Since they were undoubtedly going abroad he must look his best and decided to retrieve his fake Cartier brooch from Berington's Pawnbrokers in Westminster before returning home. He mused to himself about the journey to France, as the cab sped south towards Mayfair. Eventually he arrived at the railway station some twenty-five minutes later due to heavy traffic and instructed the cabbie to wait for him as it was still raining. At the reservations desk he booked seats for the boat train and cabins on the paddle steamer *Pride of Penge* bound for Calais, which was departing the following afternoon. Tomorrow, weather permitting, they would be able to take the air on deck and watch England's white cliffs of Dover recede into the distance, to be replaced by France's white cliffs of Cap Blanc Nez. With further train journeys to be arranged to Paris and onwards to Limoges, there would be some time to brush up on what little French he knew, which at present was limited to: 'The pen of my aunt is in the garden' and 'Granny is having a fit, go fetch a gendarme!' But there was still much to do before they commenced their travels. Packing Gridlock's belongings was always a nightmare, because he insisted on taking every conceivable thing that might prove useful, and apart from catering for Gridlock's requirements, there were arrangements to be made at home. He made a mental note for Lilly to feed Sputum daily and to look after the old place in their absence, as well as she was able. But there was still his master's craving for liquorice allsorts to consider. It was all too much.

Chapter 2

Bon voyage to 'Granchez'

The journey to Limoges by sea and rail was not without incident. Lady Bulimia Puke spent most of the Channel-crossing gazing into the detective's grey-green eye and black leather eye patch. She picked at the full English breakfast, which had been placed on the table before them. Huge waves buffeted the cross-Channel ship, and plates, cups, saucers and condiments slid from side to side as the two travellers attempted to eat. Soon the table was coated in a veneer of scrambled eggs, sausage, and the luxury of baked beans, mushrooms, porridge, soggy toast and coffee. Dabbing her mouth delicately with a serviette Bulimia attempted to remove a rasher of bacon that had slipped between her well-endowed cleavage.

"Please, my dear Lady Bulimia, allow me to assist you." Spumes leant forward, spoon in hand and attempted to procure the greasy slice that had slid even further down her décolletage. As he did so the ship rolled violently, he lost balance and fell face down into his bowl of porridge. Both parties endeavoured to clean themselves up in a dignified manner, using the table napkins provided.

"Pwray tell me Gwidlock," asked Lady Bulimia, attempting to make light of their predicament. "Why do you always wear a black leather patch over your wright eye? Is it merely an affectation, or are you indeed coverwing some dwreadful injuwry?"

"It is not always worn over my right eye, my dear lady and neither is it always of black leather," he confided. "I occasionally wear it over my left eye and sometimes even change the colour and fabric, according to the mood I am in," he jested.

"And what mood, pwray, are you in at the pwresent Gwidlock?" enquired Bulimia, coquettishly.

"At present," said Gridlock with a rakish leer, "I am most certainly in a mood for black leather!"

Bulimia blushed coyly and persisted, "But Gwidlock, why wear a patch at all?"

"It's a cunning ploy I use to confuse my enemies and would-be assassins." he replied.

"How twruly bwrilliant you are Gridlock." she sighed.

"Alas, that is only half the story." he continued looking out at the waves.

"Years ago whilst I was serving in India in the rugged region of the Bladderpur Mountains, a festering old Fakir, the guardian of a temple, apprehended me as I was inspecting the sacred statue of the She-Goddess Fatima the Fetid. For no apparent reason, he laid a dreadful curse upon me. That night, just as the Fakir prophesied, I was bitten on the rump by the dreaded poisonous Ding-el-Beri spider. As a result, I fell into a deep coma, climbed out again and ever since I've worn the patch to remind me." Overcome with emotion, he then rested his head in his hands, sobbed quietly for a moment, removed a half-eaten sausage, which had fallen into his waistcoat pocket, and began to chew on it pensively.

"You poor lamb." Bulimia whispered, with a confused look on her face for truly, she was none the wiser following the answer the great detective had provided.

As the ship rose and fell they both looked out to sea, and their eyes were directed to a windswept, dishevelled and sodden figure of a portly, ginger-moustached man attired in female clothing. The poor wretch was hanging onto the safety rail for dear life, whilst attempting to physically eject his half-digested breakfast over the side of the vessel. But unfortunately he was facing into the wind which resulted in the inevitable. Great waves almost swept the unfortunate person overboard.

As Gridlock sat back in his comfortable chair, unperturbed, he remarked, "It's certainly rum weather out there, and no mistake."

"But if I am not much mistaken, the poor man outside is your good fwriend the doctor. Oughtn't we to invite him in? He must be soaked to the skin and half-fwrozen."

"Nonsense, my dear," replied the detective as he lit a cigar and sipped his coffee. "You don't know Prunestone as well as I. Why, he likes nothing more that to pit himself against the elements. He covets the challenge, rejoices in the thrill, and revels in doing battle with the evil forces that threaten to undermine our society. The man's a true brick."

"Please don't call him names," Bulimia sighed.

"My dear lady, do not be deceived, underneath that soft feminine exterior of his there lies a heart of oak, a tough and tenacious lady-man." Barely had Gridlock finished his sentence, than another gigantic wave covered the screaming and retching Prunestone.

"Well, my dear," announced Spumes, rising unsteadily. "I can just see that we are in sight of the French coast. Come, we should prepare ourselves for the short journey to Paris."

Their journey to the French capital ran smoothly, and eventually the train pulled into the Gare Du Nord where they then hired a hansom cab to cross the city to the Gare Austerlitz. As the detective and his client boarded the carriage, a still saturated Phuckwytte attempted to join them, but his way was barred by his smiling employer.

"Sorry, old boy, you can't possibly share this cab with us, not with those dripping petticoats and all our luggage, no – best catch an omnibus." And with that, he shouted their desired destination to a disinterested cabbie, slammed the door shut, and they proceeded on their way leaving a dumb-struck Phuckwytte stranded outside of the Gare du Nord. The abandoned doctor sat on a travelling trunk in the pouring rain with the rest of the luggage, patted Ringworm the stuffed dog and contemplated his next move.

Crowds of grim-faced Parisians jostled by the solitary figure. Some shouted and cursed at him for being in their way, while others stopped and stared in disbelief, and occasionally drunks and perverts attempted to proposition him.

"Sorry, old boy, you can't possibly share this cab with us, not with
those dripping petticoats and all the luggage, no –
best catch an omnibus."

To make matters worse, whenever he opened his mouth to utter some limited French phrase he had learned at school such as, 'Help me please, the pen of my aunt is in the bathroom,' or 'Why is there an omnibus, does it come downstairs soon?' also, 'My granny is having a fit, please remove the saucepan,' he was ridiculed and taunted by passers-by with shouts of, "Go home bloody English," and "Listen to the old tart – disgusting perverts, should be locked up," and so on.

The doctor, now at his wits' end, cursed Gridlock out loud and was almost on the verge of taking the next train back to Calais when, miraculously, a horse drawn omnibus drew to a halt not ten metres from where he was sitting. Emblazoned in large letters above the cab were the magic words 'Gare d'Austerlitz'. He jumped up and down and slowly began to drag the luggage towards the bus. Immediately, two spotty-faced young urchins offered to help him.

"Oh thank you, thank you, you are too kind," he said gratefully and when juveniles had carried the baggage to the waiting bus they held out their grubby hands and demanded five francs each.

"But you didn't tell me you wanted money before," Phuckwytte complained.

"Well, we're telling you now!" came the reply. "Ten francs, or we drag it back to where it came from." Muttering under his breath, the doctor reluctantly handed over the money.

A stony-faced bus conductor now stood in his way and said with a Gallic shake of his head, "Oh no – no, no you don't, you can't put all that rubbish on my bus, not unless you pay the extra."

"Extra. What extra?" came the reply.

"Let me see now," said the sour-faced official. "One travelling trunk, three valises, golf clubs and a stuffed canine, that'll be fifteen francs plus another five for yourself – twenty francs if you please Madame!"

"Daylight robbery, that's what it is," complained the doctor. "Now I've not a centime left."

No assistance was offered as he struggled to haul the luggage aboard. When it was in place, he attempted to find a seat. Everywhere he looked he was shooed away by passengers, who were appalled at the sight of a drenched Englishman in female attire. By this time he was a sorry sight indeed. Apart from dripping water everywhere, the rain had smeared his make-up; his wig now sat at a peculiar angle; and the ostrich feathers which were once placed elegantly on his favourite hat, now drooped all over his face. He turned and noticed that at the back of the carriage there was a row of empty seats, apart from one fellow who was stretched out across the full length of the bench, and was taking huge gulps from his bottle of Pastis. He was unshaven and his clothes were ragged and unclean.

Oh well, never mind, any sport in a storm, thought Phuckwytte. He approached the bench and asked if he could sit down. The man was quite taken aback that anyone should want to sit next to him, for usually people avoided him like the plague. The bus lurched round a corner and both he and the doctor were flung backwards on to the seat.

"Mon Dieu Madame, it will be an honour to share this journey with such an elegant lady." He then offered Phuckwytte his bottle which was politely declined with a half-hearted smile.

"Allow me to introduce myself," the inebriated man slurred in his best English. "I am the famous, the renowned, Petomane. Artiste and entertainer extraordinaire."

"Pleased to meet you, I'm sure. What kind of entertainer are you exactly?"

"You mean, you 'ave not 'eard of me? Ze great Petomane? Sacre-Bleu. I 'ave performed all over Europe and in Ze best English music 'alls. I 'ave entertained royalty, I am, Madame, a musician wiz a difference, 'ow can I put it? I perform popular songs and melodies by employing ze rare anatomical gift which I 'ave been blessed with."

"Oh, you mean you are a singer – how wonderful!"

"Non, Madame, not exactly a singer. My music is not made by my vocal chords, as it were."

"Oh!" the doctor frowned. "Then where does your music come from?"

"It comes from ze place where the sun never shines, oui, down there!" and with that, the unkempt man pointed to his nether regions and laughed raucously.

"You mean that you – you interpret music by using your – your…"

"Oui – my arse, bien sur, as it 'appens I was practising my own arrangement of our national anthem 'Le Marseillaise' before you joined me. Zeese peasants 'ere zey do not appreciate ze culture, non?" The little man then smoothed back his shiny back oiled hair, combed his walrus moustache and took another gulp of Pastis and continued, "But now Le Great Le Petomane – he iz finished. Once I was the toast of Europe, but now I am nothing – too many imitators, some of zem were not genuine, and the women are worse! Zey cheat wiz bellows and clacketts hidden beneath their skirts. Now I am a lowly street performer, but sadly, ze acoustics are not so good outdoors."

Phuckwytte genuinely felt sorry for the fallen music hall star, declining his offer of a performance of 'Land of Hope and Glory'. The strange couple chatted on for the remainder of the journey and the doctor was delighted to discover that his newfound friend proved to be a expert guide on the journey through Paris.

As the carriage drew to a halt outside Austerlitz Station, Phuckwytte's companion helped him to unload his luggage and bade him, "Bonne Voyage. I shall remain 'ere and perform my repertoire outside of ze station."

The doctor glanced back to see the little man standing quite still, his legs bowed and apart, with his hands on his knees. He was surrounded by a group of Japanese tourists who were giggling as he performed 'Blow the Wind Southerly'. Glancing up at the station clock he realised that his train was about to depart, and racing to the Limoges platform as fast as he could manage, he heard the announcement for his train's departure.

Phuckwytte now raced down the platform pushing a huge baggage trolley and eventually, on his last legs, (having already worn out two pairs) he found his companions safely ensconced in a luxurious compartment, chatting contentedly. Frantically he tapped on the carriage window with his handbag, demanding admittance.

"Let me in Spumes," he cried. "Let me in for God's sake, the train is about to depart!"

Gridlock opened the window and shouted, "Don't be a fool, Prunestone, you agreed to look after the luggage and I agreed to look after our guest. The luggage van is at the other end of the train with the coal and livestock." Phuckwytte muttered something undecipherable and continued running towards the end of the platform.

"So glad I thought to put wheels on Ringworm, he's so much easier to handle now," observed Gridlock.

"Indeed, you are a kind and thoughtful fellow Mr Spumes," commented Bulimia.

The engine whistle blew and both Phuckwytte and the platform were immersed in steam. As the powerful locomotive edged forward, the doctor managed to throw the baggage into an open luggage compartment and he was now running with the train, both hands gripped firmly on the side of the door. A pair of grimy hands grabbed him and dragged him up into a dark and stinking carriage, which appeared to be full not only of luggage, but of what can only be described as 'gentlemen of the road' who had fallen on hard times. An accordionist struck up the much-loved tune '*Non, Rien de Rien*' (still to be recorded by Edith Piaf in

1960) to which the travellers sang, whistled or hummed. Phuckwytte noted that some hummed more than others. As his eyes became accustomed to the dim interior, a massive hairy and tattooed hand was thrust towards him, which he was invited to shake. It was attached to an arm that had the bulging biceps and broad shoulders of a large, tall, waxed moustachioed individual. Under his cape, he wore a sequined showman's costume, upon the chest of which was displayed an array of numerous medals, while his muscular legs were clad in silk tights, over-worn with black lacy knickers. Special leather wrestling-pumps completed the whole ensemble. Shocked by this spectacle, Phuckwytte offered his well-manicured hand, prompting the man to introduce himself.

"Ma name eez 'Marcel ze Mangler', well zat waz ma wrestling nom, but you can call me Marcel." Marcel took the doctor's hand and pressed it to his brandy-soaked lips.

"You are a preety leetle thing, tell me what are you doing 'ere. You 'ave escaped from your 'usband, perhaps?" He then slipped his huge muscular arm around the doctor's waist and whispered something in his ear. The wrestler's companions grinned and chuckled, while the doctor tried to laugh along with them, but at the same time he wondered how many bones might break if he now jumped for freedom.

Meanwhile in the more luxurious part of the train, as the detective sat contemplating the plight of the attractive woman sitting beside him, she enquired, "Pwray tell me Gwridlock, something of your past life, as we have hours of twravel ahead of us, and I would love to know something of your histowry and ancestwry. I note for instance, that you are a pwroud weawrer of the kilt. Fwrom which clan does your tartan dewrive?"

46

"Tis true," replied Gwridlock, "I am indeed a proud wearer of the kilt. Our tartan evolved by the unification of several clans: the McDonalds, the McReekies, the McAlpines not to mention the McFisheries."

"Good gwracious," gasped Bulimia. "The McFisheries too!"

"I said not to mention the McFisheries," he said abruptly and continued.

"I was born in a lowly crofter's cottage on a northerly windswept desolate rock called the Isle of Grymstone. The owner of the ruined hovel, an old gnarled crofter by the name of Leglag McKnees, was less than pleased when he discovered that Mamma and I were living under his stairs in a packing case, where we managed to survive undetected for over seven years. Despite our pathetic pleading, the farmer threw us out one dark night, when a vicious blizzard was raging. Somehow, we managed to find our way, frostbitten and exhausted, to Gridlock Hall, the ancestral seat of my father, the Eighth Laird of Gridlock, from whom my mother had escaped all those years before. After much pleading, begging and three verses of 'There's no place like home', he took us in and then forced us to become his menial servants. As a result, I became a responsible emptier and cleaner of the privvies and my poor mother was used as a char woman, and for the gathering and cutting of firewood. Not an easy task, as there were no trees on the island. She was finally given a blunt axe and a leather coracle with which to work. Our luck changed some years later, when my father died during a particularly violent attack of beriberi."

Pausing, he looked into the distance.

"My father – now what can I say about my dear old Pa? He was an accomplished miser; a bullying insensitive drunkard; a wife-beating, servant-kicking, dog-hanging beast. Apart from that, he was a self-centred, self-righteous, double-dealing, cheating rogue and a cowardly, murdering, fornicating monster. Those were his good points, but he did have a dark side as well," he confessed.

"As there were no other heirs to the estate, we became the sole inheritors of his vast organic haggis factory, his castle and all the land thereabout which was populated by an assortment of peasants. In addition, my father left me his private collection of French postcards and backdated copies of *Whiplash Weekly*, which I've kept in the bottom drawer."

"Oh dear," responded the startled lady, as Gridlock fervently reminisced.

"After a spell at Charterhouse Public School, I gained a place at Edinburgh University where I obtained a first grade in the study of the 'Psychology of the Criminal Mind', along with flower arranging and Origami. On leaving University I opted for a life of adventure and joined the military, becoming a Captain in the Royal Highland Foot and Mouth Regiment. Naturally, I was attached to intelligence. Ultimately, after four years' service, fighting for Queen and Empire, I returned to 'Old Blighty', set up digs in Baker Street and became the greatest, and possibly the only private detective England has." he boasted.

"Indeed Gridlock," agreed Bulimia. "Your name is known throughout the length and bwreadth of Deptford. It is because of your wreputation that we called upon you for help."

"And you could not have made a finer choice my dear lady, I can assure you," he beamed with self-importance.

At this point Gridlock was interrupted by a distant voice announcing in an Italian accent, "Smok'a kippas, smok'a kippas, come an' try my smok'a kippa baguettes." The announcement became louder as the vendor lurched down the corridor towards their compartment. The door opened and there stood a four foot high, black-moustachioed, golden ear-ringed, scarlet bandanna-clad, velvet waist-coated, stripy-pantalooned, black leather-booted seller of smoked kipper baguettes. He was bearing a tray laden with his merchandise with the words: 'Alfredo's Smok'a Kippa Baguettas' across the front.

"Eh, Signor en Signorita, you wanna try Alfredo's smok'a kippas wid or widout oregano. Dey is delicioso!" smiled the height-challenged Latino.

"I must say Gwidlock, I do feel a little peckish, I haven't had kippers for ages," remarked Bulimia.

"Then you shall have one dear lady, and so shall I by gad! Two of your finest smoked kipper baguettes and pronto!"

"Two smok'a kippa baguettes an' pronto coming up."

"How much is that?"

"Two centimes Signor," the vendor grinned, displaying a row of flashing gold teeth. He carefully wrapped the baguettes in an Italian copy of *The News of the World*, took the cash, slammed the door and disappeared as quickly as he had made his entrance.

"Hmm…" muttered Gridlock. "Curious little fellow. Old 'Johnny Foreigner' never ceases to amaze me."

"I'm famished," said Bulimia as she hurriedly opened her baguette to observe the contents. To her surprise, no trace of kipper was to be found. In its place was a folded, olive oil and oregano-stained circus programme, on the back of which was a badly handwritten message: 'No 1 crossis 'The Great Castrato' an'a live. U haf not leaf money in Savoy ladis lav as constructed. Giv monie now or u wil pay'a the konsiquincies. U haf bin warn.' Lady Bulimia dropped her baguette and stared at Gridlock, imploring him with her eyes to say something. This prompted the detective to open his baguette whereupon he took out yet another stained, folded circus programme also with a message on the back, which read: 'Sam'a for u 2 pizza face, kip yor big'a nose out'.

"Damn and blast, what a fool I've been," he admitted. "Forgive me dear lady, but your exquisite charm and beauty seem to have detracted me from my duty. I now realise we have been followed ever since we boarded the train at Victoria. I recall now a man at least seven feet tall by the name of Alf, selling eel pie and mash on the platform. Then on the ferry an enormously fat waiter by the name of Alfred served us breakfast. On the train from Calais to Paris a painfully thin Arab named Al-Fred was serving goat's genitalia and couscous. And now, the midget Alfredo and his smoked kippers. If I am not very much mistaken, they are all the same man."

"But how could that possibly be?" enquired Bulimia nervously.

"They all had gold teeth," replied the detective.

"But they were all completely different, how could it possibly be the same man?"

"Trick of the light," said Gridlock casually. "Simply a trick of the light... that and their mastery of disguise."

At that moment, the train slowed down and pulled into the Gare de Limoges. Gridlock rose from his seat, lit his meerschaum, quickly put on his deerstalker and donned his greatcoat, woollen scarf and mittens.

"You look magnificent," swooned Bulimia, "but aren't you hot in that attire?"

"One cannot be too careful," he replied. "Come, there is no time to lose. Let us find Prunestone and proceed to our destination."

For some minutes they waited on the platform, but the doctor failed to appear.

"Strange," he noted. "Prunestone is a man of infinite punctuality; let us see if we can find him." They walked briskly back up towards the baggage compartment, and on peering into the darkness of the end carriage, they saw a figure struggling and rolling across the floor. Climbing in and lighting a match, they were amazed at the sight that confronted them.

"By God, it's Prunestone! The poor wretch has been bound and gagged!" Spumes whipped out his trusty pocket knife and in no time he had cut the doctor free. He then removed a baguette from his friend's mouth, opened it and took out yet another discoloured circus programme, (this time soiled with French mustard) which advertised 'The Magnificent Marcel' strongman, wrestler and itinerant part-time scaffolder. On the back was badly written: 'Forgive me doctor, my Cherie, 'ave no choice as ze flick is after me and I must 'ide. Sorry I tie you. Will return an' find you, my leetle English rosebud. Much amour, Marcel.' Gridlock eyed the doctor suspiciously, while Phuckwytte coughed nervously and muttered something about duty and sacrifice for one's 'Queen and Country'.

Within minutes they had unloaded their baggage, and were now stood in the foyer of La Gare de Limoges. Unfortunately no immediate carriages were to be found, but eventually after some bargaining they were able to procure a passing hay cart, for the next stage of their journey and thankfully, the travellers climbed aboard with their luggage. The driver, indistinguishable beneath a dark cloak, enquired where exactly they wanted to go.

"A small hamlet called Granchez, near the village of Lozenge, my good man. For it is both a rest home and an asylum for the mentally infirm," replied Phuckwytte.

"Oui Madame." The driver then shook his head, crossed himself, cracked his whip and they were off.

"I say Spumes," remarked Phuckwytte, "did you notice the driver's teeth?"

"Can't say I did," retorted his master indifferently, as he stifled a yawn and settled down amongst the hay.

"All gold," muttered Phuckwytte to himself. "I swear every single tooth was gold. How very curious."

As the overworked old nag was whipped into an unheard of frenzy, it managed to reach the staggering speed of four miles an hour. The journey north seemed to take forever, due to the cart being overladen with luggage, along with the occupants who were precariously balanced on a mountain of hay. Their driver, having limited navigational skills, proceeded east, then south, then west. After some hours he eventually found his bearings (which he tossed in the air and caught), and continued north again. As they proceeded, their nostrils were filled with the noxious garlic and onion aromas that were being emitted by their chauffeur, which he blamed on the poor horse. Their progress was further hampered by Phuckwytte's continual demands for the cart to stop so that he might relieve himself, for his experiences on the journey by train from Paris had not helped his already weak bladder. The final leg of the trip by train had been a complete catastrophe for him, since he'd been forced repeatedly to dance a 'gentlemen's excuse me' with the Mangler and his companions. The strong-man was truly smitten by Phuckwytte's alluring make-up and ginger moustache. Phuckwytte had prayed continually that the accordionist would not include a slow waltz in his limited repertoire, and his final act of humiliation was to be forced into performing a lively variation of the 'Can-Can' after which he was trussed up like a chicken, bound and gagged.

Now in the cold light of the summer moon, while crickets chirped in the hedgerows and herds of Limousin cattle gorged themselves on the lush grass, inevitably resulting in them quietly releasing the digested contents in their stomachs over the fields, the hay cart driver turned and smiled a familiar gold-toothed smile. *Was it the same man who had thrust the baguette into his mouth*, he wondered? If so, he was relieved that it was only his mouth that had suffered that indignity. His whalebone corset and strengthened undergarments had seen to that. Through countless deserted villages and hamlets they passed, the driver complaining about the smell of the horse, the horse complaining about the smell of the driver, Bulimia complaining about her hay fever and Phuckwytte complaining about his bladder. Eventually the overpowering stench of raw onion and garlic produced a volatile concoction which ignited in a powerful explosion, as Gridlock unthinkingly struck a match to light his pipe, causing the horse to bolt, and the driver (who was still holding the reins) to be dragged off into the night. The cart then ignited into a ball of fire, lighting up the surrounding countryside.

Gridlock was incensed due to this ridiculous incident, not to mention the inconvenience and damage it had incurred. Above all else, his reputation had been severely dented.

"Damned Frogs." he cursed loudly, in a fit of pique, apologising to Bulimia afterwards for his momentary lapse of decorum. To add insult to injury, he had found the charred remains of his faithful stuffed dog Ringworm.

"Look at the state of me," sobbed Phuckwytte, his dress torn, wig scorched and his face blackened. He hobbled about on one high heel and complained, "I've broken a bloody nail too."

"Shut up and collect what's left of our luggage," Gridlock responded crossly, for he was now in no mood for the doctor's whinging.

Bulimia confessed, "I'm sorrwy to have got you both into this terrwible mess; it was not my intention…"

"Madam, please don't blame yourself," interrupted the detective, "It just goes to show you how fiendish and unscrupulous these people are."

Somewhat shaken by their experience, they gathered the burnt remains of their belongings and continued on foot the short distance into the next tiny hamlet of St Cretin-le-Stench (population twelve and a half) where they were able by sign language to procure beds for the night. The only hostelry available was a converted packing shed, which was owned by a gentleman by the name of Periquenx Grotts, who like the town in the Dordogne, had a reputation for Roman remains and pate de foie gras, this delicacy his loving wife Celine administered to his nether regions by candlelight every night, as she lullabyed him with rural folksongs. He had the usual mouthful of blackened teeth, a squint and the distinctive appearance of a stunted gargoyle, obviously the unfortunate result of centuries of inbreeding.

The following morning Gridlock's usual nine and a half press-ups were followed by a short interlude on the violin in a cold bath. He finally met up with the others in the small sparse dining room in the main house. Our companions seated themselves on a rickety old collection of worm-eaten chairs, arranged haphazardly around a filthy, grease-coated table and waited for their worm-eaten, filthy and grease-coated landlord to serve breakfast. Eventually, Monsieur Grotts appeared at the kitchen door bearing a tray upon which two stale and badly burnt baguettes, a pot of stewed brown liquid which passed as lukewarm coffee and a bowl of steaming Andouillette sausages, (a stinky French delicacy made from pigs' rectums) were displayed. The travellers studied the grisly meal before them with a mixture of disgust and apprehension, but hunger forced them to partake of the culinary delights. The rock hard and blackened bread resisted all attempts at being cut with knives, and it was unceremoniously beaten over the table until broken. The pieces that remained on the table were then soaked in bowls of the lukewarm coloured water until they were almost soft enough to chew. The Andouillettes, not surprisingly, remained untouched. As Bulimia dabbed her mouth delicately with the hem of Phuckwytte's dress she noticed in the corner of the room next to the window a portly gentleman, who observed the companions intently over the top of his newspaper. His sallow complexion reminded her of putty by moonlight, and this was enhanced by his jet-black eyes, hair and moustache. He was impeccably dressed in black bowler hat, morning coat, waistcoat with watch chain and a pair of gold-rimmed pince-nez glasses were perched on the end of his nose. The upper part of his body appeared to be perfectly normal, but his little legs dangled over the edge of his chair with his feet at least a foot from the ground. He gave Bulimia a long and suggestive wink, at which she affected to be embarrassed.

From upstairs came the sound of raised voices as footsteps began to descend the wooden stairs. The noise of pushing, shoving and swearing could now be clearly heard. Our travellers stopped chewing on their petit dejeuner and looked up at the stairs as three unlikely looking characters stumbled down in some disorder.

"Bloody attention seeker, that's what you are," bawled one of the men. "Cutting your bloody ear off just as we are about to commence our long awaited painting expedition, sodding exhibitionist, all you ginger-haired bastards are the same!"

A red-bearded man clutching a blood stained towel to his ear replied, "You callous, uncaring, self-obsessed, disease-ridden bastard. Why don't you sod off back to Tahiti and infect the whole bloody island. We all know what you get up to over there – and painting hasn't got much to do with it, you degenerate swine!" By this time the men had reached the foot of the staircase and the third man, attired in paint-splattered artist's smock complete with large black beret and sporting a long and luxuriant beard, attempted to calm the situation.

"Now, now, please, gentlemen. We are all supposed to be good friends, fellow artists, about to embark upon an epic painting adventure."

"Huh!" replied the swarthy and bad-tempered member of the group. "All you'll get out of him are bloody sunflowers and maybe a cornfield or two – if you're lucky."

"Yes, yes," replied the peacekeeper. "I myself intend to finish my series of haystacks."

"That's all very well," said the one-eared artist, "but why do you paint them over and over again?"

"Because the bloody haystack keeps moving, that's why," came the irritated reply. He then spotted the dapper little man in the corner. "Ah! There you are my friend, up early to make a start on these wonderful landscapes of La Creuse?"

"Bollocks to that!" came the retort. "I'll leave all the chocolate box stuff to you chaps. Me, I'm going off to the nearest knocking-shop to sample some real life! Monsieur Grotts will direct me there and he assures me that I shall not be disappointed. Great strong curvy arsed rural lasses in abundance – can't wait! Stuff landscapes!"

"You cunning little bastard," replied the short-tempered man. "Mind if I join you?"

"No, no, no," asserted the bushy-bearded dauber. "We are here to paint the countryside, and that's what we will do."

"Very well, but can we visit the bordello after?" the small man enquired.

"If you must, but I myself shall continue with my haystacks throughout the night."

"Moron," muttered the painter of naked young native girls.

The red-bearded man dabbed at his ear with a towel and asked the master of the house is he could have a bowl of hot water. "I've had an accident you see, and I've cut my ear off."

"I don't care if you've cut yer bleedin' weddin' tackle off," replied Grotts. "Just don't drip blood all over my nice antique oak table. Bloody artists! Now, what would you gents care for?"

"For you to put some actual coffee in the pot for a change and a hammer and chisel to break up that excuse for bread you serve." Grotts swore under his breath and returned to his kitchen.

Phuckwytte, who had been listening intently to their conversation, waddled over to where they sat, curtsied and introduced himself.

"Forgive this intrusion but I couldn't help overhearing that you gentlemen are all artists – how fascinating! I myself dabble in watercolours. In fact I have a small sketch book with me and I would be honoured if you would give me your opinions on my style and technique." With that, the doctor fumbled in his handbag and produced a small pink-coloured pad. He offered it to the company who in turn passed it around.

"As you can see, my preferred subject is the study of flowers: there is my first attempt – a dandelion, and this one is a daisy. You will also find buttercups and violets. But my pièce de résistance is on the last page, a foxglove – what a challenge that was!" One by one the painters studied the clumsy and badly drawn attempts, looked at each other in disbelief and tried desperately to suppress the laughter that might have erupted at any second.

"Umm, umm, interesting!"

"Ahh, such style, such subtlety!"

"Well, well, well!"

"Sacre-bleu, I have never seen the like!" were some of the comments passed around. These were followed by a long silence as the book was handed back to a beaming Phuckwytte. Gridlock realised that he should put an end to this embarrassing episode. He stood slowly adjusting his kilt, sporran, eye patch and monocle and walked towards the gathering. Coughing nervously to clear his throat, he glanced around at the assembly, grabbed Phuckwytte's arm firmly and commenced his apology.

"Gentlemen, please, I beg you to forgive my friend's intrusion, but the poor fellow suffers from delusions of grandeur. Today, as you can see he is 'The Great Artist', a female one at that! Last week he was an eminent surgeon, and the week before, 'The Emperor of China' and so on, I think you get the picture?"

The men nodded gravely, and as the doctor struggled to remonstrate, Gridlock increased the pressure on his friend's arm and continued, "We are on our way to Lozenge where an eminent psychiatrist will attempt to cure him of his delusions and of his abnormal dress fetish." Phuckwytte was by now furious, but Gridlock increased his vice-like grip and his companion was silenced.

"Lozenge you say?" replied the artist with the black beret. "What a coincidence, we ourselves are setting out for that very village this morning, we wish to avail ourselves of the magnificent scenery thereabouts for we are members of the Lozenge Impressionist Painters' Society, or LIPS, for short."

"No, but I have heard of the French Artists of Rural Themes, better known as the FARTS…"

"Ah yes, they are great rivals of ours along with the Creuse Regional Arts for Paupers' Society, or CRAPS as they are better known… anyhow, you are most welcome to join us on our journey there. We have a horse-drawn charabanc at our disposal and there is plenty of room for you all."

"Most kind, most kind," replied Gridlock. "Let us gather together our things at once." Bulimia however, much to the detective's irritation remained seated at the artists' table and was now revelling in the attention she was receiving from them, as they fawned over her in an openly lecherous fashion.

"Mon Dieu – what a beauty you are, such eyes, such a figure, such skin, I must paint you!"

"Non, non, me first, I insist. Here is the address of my studio in Paris, I will immortalise your beauty on canvas!"

"Madame, such beauty should be painted by a Master such as myself – I wish to paint you naked by a haystack in moonlight!"

"Sacre Bleu!" shouted out the one-eared painter. "Do not listen to these amateurs. Come with me to the sunflower fields of Southern France – aaaahh! This bloody ear is giving me gip…"

"Of course," Bulimia replied, "I will try to accommodate you all – as it were! But first things first." She then hoisted her dress to reveal the full length of her shapely leg, placed her foot on a chair, took off her bootee, rolled down her silk stocking and removed it to bandage the head of the one-eared artist.

Gridlock was now beside himself with jealousy, which he attempted to suppress by cramming liquorice into his mouth and grinning insanely. "Come, my dear Bulimia," he lisped through a mouthful of black goo. "Let us go and prepare ourselves for the journey." He took her arm as she smiled seductively at the salivating men who attempted to remove their tongues from the greasy breakfast table.

Within the hour, the travellers had seated themselves on the charabanc, when an undignified scuffle broke out among the artists as they attempted to gain a place next to the radiant Bulimia. A sulking Phuckwytte sat next to a brooding Gridlock as the coachman cracked his whip. After two hours of bone-shaking torture, on hard wooden-slatted seats, their journey was completed as they reached a lopsided sign by a crossroads, which read: 'Granchez – Gateway to Paradise – Lozenge 1.5 km'. The painters now fell over each other in trying to help with Bulimia's luggage. Thank you's and goodbye's were exchanged and the artists took full advantage to grope and slobber over their newfound muse. The three then made for their new destination; Gridlock at the front, hopping on one leg, black of mood and countenance; Bulimia following, whilst still turning to wave and blow kisses to her retreating admirers; and lastly, a cursing and red-faced Phuckwytte, who struggled on frantically with all their luggage.

With the sun now low on the horizon and with a slight chill in the air, their hopes were finally raised by the pleasant outside appearance of a typical rustic stone farmhouse. It nestled in charming surroundings of natural beauty comprising of an attached barn with outbuildings in three acres of mature garden and lower pasture. The welcoming sign on the building announced: 'The Auberge de Granchez' under which was handwritten: 'Creative care for the certified in the community' and under that: 'Please wipe your feet, nose and anything else you've forgotten!' Gridlock pulled the lavatory chain doorbell and nothing happened. He then thumped on the door with his fist, nearly breaking his fingers in the process and was nursing his injury, when at last they heard a shuffling from within. A voice said, "Le chèque est dans la poste."

"What?" said Gridlock.

"The cheque's in the post."

"Answer this door at once!" Gridlock shouted.

"You're not those bloody Jehovah's Witnesses again are yer?"

"No." was the unanimous reply. Reluctantly, the door was unbolted and before them stood the proprietor. He was clad in a beekeeper's hat and his raffia night attire revealed a pair of bandy legs in gaiters and galoshes. Suddenly his spouse appeared, sporting a homemade hat from old newspapers, an ill-fitting gymslip and over-sized woollen socks, held up by a pair of her husband's braces.

"Who the 'ell is it?" she asked. Complementing this bizarre fashion statement, was the fact that they were both wearing boxing gloves.

"What'cher want?" enquired the voice from behind the protective gauze.

"We're from England," Phuckwytte announced.

"Don't come to me wiv your troubles mate," their host replied as he took off his hat. They explained who they were and the owner's mood at once changed, welcoming them and bidding them to enter and sit while Phuckwytte struggled in with their bags.

"Welcome to our 'umble abode," greeted Reginald Spiggott, holding out a gloved hand to be shaken. "My name's Reginald and this 'ere's my dear wife and medical assistant Ethel."

She responded with a, "Charmed I'm sure," along with a curtsey, which was repeated in turn by Phuckwytte.

"Of course you already know Lady Puke," introduced the detective.

"Glad to welcome you again, your Ladyship," they responded.

"Would you care to partake of some light refreshment before you retire?" enquired Eth.

"Splendid," returned Gridlock, and Eth disappeared into the kitchen, quickly returning with a tray of tea and homemade biscuits. "We are most grateful for your having us to stay at such short notice, and we are sorry to arrive at such a late hour," the detective apologised.

"Oh please don't be alarmed. We've just been administering the patients' medication. It 'elps them to sleep if you knock 'em out," Eth admitted. The guests were then handed candles with which to go to bed.

"Aren't you going to light them?" enquired Bulimia.

"No, they seem to last so much longer unlit," explained Reg as they then fumbled, stumbled and crashed their way upstairs in the dark with their luggage.

"Oh please don't be alarmed, we've just been administering the patients' medication, it 'elps them to sleep if you knock 'em out."

Chapter 3

Interrogation, elimination and infatuation

Gridlock woke uneasily to a loud snoring, emanating from a body next to him, and discovered that Phuckwytte had been sleepwalking again.

"Get out of my bed you bloody idiot!" he shouted, kicking the doctor in the crotch which caused him to howl with pain and to make rapidly for his own room. After a hearty breakfast they relaxed in the large living room in front of a roaring open log fire that seemed a little strange, since it was a sweltering hot day outside. Following a lengthy amount of pleasantries, Gridlock took off his smoking jacket, loosened his tie and collar and then began to converse in earnest.

"I have been instructed by my client here, Lady Puke, to investigate as to who is attempting to blackmail her and her husband, since their brief stay with you some time ago."

"I trust you're not insinuating that either of us, or our staff and patients are responsible? We keep a tight ship; don't count our chickens before they are hatched; a stitch in time saves nine; and a rolling stone gathers no moss. I trust that I make myself clear?"

"As mud," replied Gridlock continuing, "We have had the unfortunate experience of being followed from London by criminals who have appeared in many shapes and guises, all of whom seem to suffer from some form of flatulence."

"Most of the locals in this area have the same misfortune, in fact the region is famed for it," answered Reg proudly.

Gridlock continued undeterred, "The other possible link appears to be illiterate messages written on outdated circus programmes, demanding substantially large sums of money from my client." By now everyone was so uncomfortably hot that they had thrown caution to the wind and were stripped down to their underwear.

"There has been a written threat from someone who calls himself 'The Great Castrato', and also another individual by the name of 'Marcel the Mangler', who has made undesirable advances to my associate Doctor Prunestone here. They were undesirable weren't they?"

"Very," answered Phuckwytte blushing.

"There's no accountin' for taste," remarked Reg eyeing the crestfallen doctor who at last jumped to his defence, voicing his objections.

"The brute made the most undesirable advances and left a message in a baguette," he tried to explain but was interrupted.

"Might we all continue this enquiry outside in the garden, since it is such a lovely day?" suggested Gridlock.

"By all means, please follow me," said Reg as he showed them out onto the lawn in their undergarments. Their hats, however, were kept in place, as a precaution against rain.

After a few moments Reg asked, "But what brings you 'ere to 'Granchez'?"

Gridlock referred to his notes and explained. "It appears that during my client's honeymoon stay here, there seems to have been a series of, shall we say, odd occurrences that took place during the night. These took the form of a loud scream followed by an excerpt of classical music expertly played on your Steinway, and last, but not least, an incontinent elephant."

"Don't forget the Havana cigar and the pickled hewring," reminded Bulimia.

"Quite," said Gridlock.

"May I ask what form of medication you're takin'?" enquired Reg.

"I'm not taking any bloody medication!" replied Gridlock sharply.

"You could have fooled me," their host chuckled. At this moment the conversation was interrupted by Eth shouting through a speaking trumpet, announcing that it was 'medicine time' for the patients. A queue was instantly formed as if by magic, at the dispensing counter, to receive their regular daily doses.

"Please excuse me, duty calls," said Reg and left the pair to continue his responsibility of running the household.

Gridlock endeavoured to regain his composure. "I don't trust that man. He appears to be hiding something," he said suspiciously.

"He seems quite helpful to me," observed Phuckwytte.

"You mark my words, there's more to this than meets the eye Prunestone."

"You should know," said the doctor pointing at his master's eye patch.

"Don't be flippant!" remarked Gridlock as he moved his eye patch to his other eye,

"We will have to interview everyone connected with this institution to establish whose criminal mind is at work."

"But how will we be able to tell?" asked the doctor.

"Process of elimination my dear Prunestone, process of elimination."

"Good show old man!" congratulated Phuckwytte.

"That is why I remain the detective genius, alert and suspicious of everyone, keen of eye, albeit a patched one, and you dear Phuckwytte, you remain a complete berk."

"That's very kind of you to say so," thanked Phuckwytte, knowing that any acknowledgement or false praise, however unflattering, was better than none.

"Before I attempt to interview patients and staff I suggest that we take a stroll around the grounds in order to familiarise ourselves with the lie of the land. But before we do, I strongly recommend that you change into something a little more masculine, since we don't want to frighten the patients do we?" Visibly wounded, Prunestone minced dejectedly to his quarters in order to carry out his master's wishes.

The detective then opened his worn leather bag in order to check that all his apparatus was present and correct. He removed each item, which he thought might be of some use and put them one by one into his pocket. One piece of old string; one used handkerchief with a knot in it (but he couldn't remember what for); one blunt penknife; one pot of haemorrhoid cream; one box of half used matches; one cracked magnifying glass and an old copy of the limited edition of *Flagellation Can Be Fun* magazine in a plain brown wrapper; half an ounce of liquorice allsorts; and finally, a pair of industrial strength brown flannel drawers. Experience had taught him to take no chances. Lighting up his pipe he contemplated the buildings around him. A wisp of smoke hurriedly escaped from the bowl. Immediately he re-inserted a fresh wisp and then attempted to negotiate the garden hammock, misjudged his momentum and promptly fell out again into the herbaceous border, nearly swallowing his treasured meerschaum. He was plucking sprigs of lavender from his hat when Prunestone appeared awkwardly, apparelled in a hotchpotch collection of clothing, crowned with a moleskin bowler hat, three sizes too big, which partly covered his eyes and made his ears look even larger than usual. Snatches of his pink and lilac lace bodice peeped out from the ill-fitting tweed waistcoat, which matched his greatcoat and knickerbockers. His heavy woollen socks were tucked, not into the usual stout, hardwearing walking boots of a country gentleman; but instead, his appearance was completed with a dainty pair of high-heeled bootees affected by ladies of high fashion.

Gridlock drew on his pipe and blew a dark cloud of black shag smoke into the doctor's face and remarked cruelly, "I see that the circus is in town again Prunestone."

This insensitive remark caused Phuckwytte to retaliate. "I've done my best and if that's not good enough, I'll immediately return to 'Blighty'."

"Only joking, old bean," said the detective, patting Phuckwytte on the back. "You look splendid. Ah, here's Spiggott," he observed. "Perhaps if you are not too busy, you could give us a short guided tour of your premises?"

Their balding host adjusted his black beret with shoulder length horse-hair attached, and agreed to take the two investigators around Granchez.

"I fink we'll commence wiv the Gymnasium and recreation area," he said, in his somewhat self-important manner. He took a large tricolour handkerchief from the pocket of his painter's smock, blew his nose on it and then used it to clean the largest pair of spectacles Gridlock had ever seen, the lenses being incredibly thick.

"May I presume to ask why you're dressed in such a fashion?" asked Gridlock, "You look every inch the French Paysan, even down to your wooden clogs and your huge false waxed handlebar moustache."

Reg grinned and retorted with a Gallic shrug, "Ah well, yer see, some of the frenchies round 'ere ain't too keen on us old anglaise, so Eth and me decided to hintegrate an' go native, as it were. Works a treat. Fools those froggy idiots who really believe we wanna turn français, gawd 'elp us." Gridlock thought this remark somewhat callous of Reg, since he had elected to move from the 'Old Country' and set up in business there. Selecting a huge iron key from the dozen or so that were hanging around his neck, their host proceeded to open the great barn door.

It opened to a gloomy stone interior, lit by a couple of oil lamps, and was empty of furniture, apart from a wind-up cylinder phonograph on an old table, which was playing a cracked and barely audible recording of a French choir singing 'Oh, for the wings of a dove'. In the centre of the barn was Madame Spiggott, resplendent in her Paysan costume, although the false moustache looked rather incongruous. Standing forlornly around her in a circle was a group of dejected-looking patients, clad in grey smocks. As choreographer she was enthusiastically demonstrating how to express oneself freely, and with gay abandon. Unfortunately, at this point the patient in charge of the music changed the cylinder recording to the 1812 overture and all hell broke loose. In the ensuing scuffle Ethel Spiggott, dance mistress extraordinaire, was knocked to the ground and trampled upon by the now frantically excited patients in her care. At this, an agitated Reg blew his whistle and shouted through Eth's megaphone, "Music off please, thank you, dance over, music off."

Several menacing male and female nurses appeared from the shadows and began to restrain the ebullient performers. Eth struggled to her feet as gracefully as possible, brushed herself down, replaced her false teeth, which had been knocked out during the exercise, and said cheerfully, "Well now, that didn't go down too badly did it? But perhaps next time, we'll try them wiv a little Swan Lake!"

"Why do you call this a gymnasium, when there is not one item of equipment to be seen?" enquired the doctor.

"Crikey!" declared the dance mistress. "You've just seen wot's 'appened wivout any apparatus. Gawd knows what would 'appen if we 'ad any. Nah, free expression is wot they needs."

"What exactly do you mean by 'free expression'?" enquired Gridlock.

"Why, we give them the opportunity to dance and get exercise twice a week, ain't that right Reg?"

"Yes, my little gherkin. Yer see gentlemen, little Eth 'ere knows best. She done a three month part-time course on the causes of bed-wetting and the psychology of the criminal mind at 'Ackney Polytechnic. Didn't yer, my little pickled onion? Passed wiv honours she did, made me right proud."

"And what, pray, are your qualifications Mr Spiggott?" asked the perturbed doctor.

"Ah, now, let me see… Where shall I begin? I done a postal do-it-yerself course on self-defence and restraint techniques. I'm a self-taught expert on the appliance of electric shock treatment and I've written a thesis on 'The benefits of sex education combined with practical massage when applied to young female patients'," he proudly boasted. "All this along with my experience as a gas fitter and sanitary engineer make me more than qualified to run this establishment."

"Quite, quite," answered the doctor in an alarmed tone.

"Right then," said Reg. "Let us proceed wiv the tour, gentlemen. 'Ere we 'av the washing and bathing facilities."

"But it's just a hose connected to a tap and a tin bath."

"That's right," said Reg. "We believe in a Spartan existence 'ere. The latrine arrangements are at the bottom of the field down there," he pointed casually.

"Where?" enquired Phuckwytte, "I'm sorry but I see no buildings."

"Quite right doc. We believe in the fresh air approach, yer see."

"And we do grow some lovely veggies," piped in Ethel. The rest of the tour proved equally dismal in that the lessons taught were: oakum picking in the recreation wing; potato picking, for farm studies; and nose picking in solitary confinement. The patients' quarters, had hot and cold running water, mostly down the walls and they were allowed to keep the odd vermin as pets.

After a brief and disturbing visit to the kitchens that doubled up as the medical room, the increasingly suspicious detective and his colleague decided to commence their interviews. Reg allotted them an outbuilding, a corrugated iron lean-to smoking room, so called because it was there that Eth smoked her herrings and on some occasions her cannabis too. Gridlock stood in authority ready to make use of his razor sharp mind in his questioning, while his associate, equipped with his notepad and pencil, sat at a makeshift desk, which consisted of two tea chests with an old door atop. A sinister member of staff whose teeth seemed to flash as he spoke, ushered in the first interviewee – a tiny mouse-like middle-aged gentleman who hopped in and sat down before them. He twitched and attempted to cross and un-cross his leg with difficulty, since he (like poor Lilly) had only the one and he continuously stared at his inquisitors with tiny piercing dark eyes.

"Fritz Shortarshe Von Strumphe at your service," announced the waxed moustachioed unidexter with a lisp, spraying the pair with a vile-smelling substance projected from the gaps in his rotting teeth. Gridlock and Phuckwytte wiped their faces in unison and commenced the questioning.

"What was your profession before you became a patient, Herr Von Strumphe?" enquired the detective.

"I voss an inventor," answered the little German.

"And what, pray have you invented?" asked the doctor.

"In my time I haff invented many sings, but ze invention for which I am most proud iz zer vistling toupee und ze self-adjustink singing vig. I vas zer sole maker und supplier to zer Royal House of Hapsburg und many follically challenged aristocrats of zer Austro-Hungarian Empire."

"I see," replied Phuckwytte, seeing nothing.

"Zer talkink beard und zer vispering moustache vere not so popular, but I am at present vorking on a choral arrangement for nasal, ear und under-arm hairs."

"Quite so, quite so," the worried doctor uttered whilst stealing a glance at an equally anxious Gridlock who then asked, "Tell me, Von Strumphe, does the following description mean anything to you? A three-legged, cigar smoking elephant that loves to play classical music on the piano?"

The little man twitched uncontrollably, rolled his eyes and uttered, "Ah zoh, zer old elephant trick ya? You vont catch Von Strumphe so easily. Ya is true, I kept such a three-legged elephant called Tripod, but zat is all in zer past. I vos merely helping him vis his incontinence und smokink problem vis hypnosis. Von day he came to my room, und tossed a smoked kipper at me, passed vind most violently und zen disappeared." The interviewers looked startled.

"Zer rest as zay say is history, und I have not seen him since." At this, Von Strumphe broke down, fell to the floor and began to chew the leg of the chair.

"Mein Gott, I miss zat Tripod, he vos my only friend."

"Thank you for your co-operation Mr Strumphe, we have finished with our questioning," announced Gridlock and Reg shouted, "Matron!" which prompted a hefty nurse to appear, holding a pink angora straitjacket, which she applied to the one-legged unfortunate and led him, whimpering, from the room.

"What do you make of that Gridlock?" asked the bemused doctor.

"Obviously a highly intelligent, if eccentric character, he is surely telling the truth, in fact, as I recall, a distant cousin of mine bought a whistling toupee in Vienna with the name 'Von

Strumphe' sewn into the lining. Unfortunately for him it only whistled Wagner's *Ride of the Valkyries* and had a habit of doing so of its own accord, which played havoc with his love life.

"Next!" demanded Gridlock. The door opened to reveal a huge female somewhat larger than the opening itself. With the help of Gridlock and Phuckwytte pulling in front and two nurses pushing from behind, they managed to squeeze the patient through. The detective cast his hawk-like eye over the Neanderthal form in front of him and concluded that something was not quite right. Was it the thick black stubble on the chin, the broken nose perhaps, the wiry black hair protruding from her bodice and wrists, the tattoos on her hands and neck, or was it the size fifteen hobnail boots? Nevertheless, the sackcloth dress hung like a curtain and her golden hair fell in ringlets about her shoulders.

"Name please," enquired the detective.

"Grizelda," answered the patient in a gruff deep voice.

"Grizelda who?"

"Grizelda Groinstrain." At this, Phuckwytte began to laugh hysterically but not for long. A huge hand shot forward and grabbed him by the throat, pulled him across the desk until he was face to face with Mademoiselle Groinstrain.

"Now, leesten 'ere you leetle Engleesh pig, show some respect or I will rip your silly 'ed off and stuff it up your arse, comprenez?"

"C... comprenez," stammered the doctor who was by now purple in the face.

"Let him go, you harridan!" cried Gridlock, "I'll have you know that I am a black belt in Origami and a green belt in flower arranging."

Suddenly, Grizelda's expression softened as she stared into Phuckwytte's eyes. "Sacre Bleu, Mon dieu," she exclaimed. "Eet iz ma leetle English rosebud, I 'ave been waiting for you, leetle one, but why are you dressed as a man? You look ridicule n'est pas?" Prunestone's face had now changed from purple to dark blue for the huge hands were still clasped firmly around his throat.

"Please release your hands!" he squeaked.

Gridlock had now adopted the stance of a prizefighter, both fists clenched firmly in front of his face as he danced about on the spot shouting, "Come on you cowardly Frenchie, come on, show me what you're made of. I'll have you know that I've boxed for the Dagenham Devil's Athletic Club, what do you think of that eh?" he taunted, and threw a feeble left jab in Grizelda's direction. His fist was caught however in her huge hand while her other let go of Phuckwytte's throat and he lifted Gridlock clean off his feet propelling him through the doorway. As the detective made his exit horizontally, his foot caught the inside of the doorframe and the flimsy construction collapsed in a heap over Groinstrain, dislodging her golden ringlets and revealing a large bald head with the word 'Mum' badly tattooed on her, or rather now his forehead.

"Marcel," exclaimed the traumatised doctor. "What are you doing here?"

"I came 'ere for you ma leetle one and 'ave thought of nothing else. I even volunteered to enrol as a female patient until you arrived, I am so 'appy."

"But I am a man," replied Phuckwytte. "Don't you understand?"

"So am I ma cherie. No-one is perfect," replied the Mangler as four nurses wrestled him to the ground and subdued the brute with a massive dose of horse tranquilliser. He was then dragged back anaesthetised to his cell.

As their makeshift interview room had now collapsed, the remainder of the questioning took place outside and the rest of the patients were questioned one by one. And what an odd assortment they were. Clothilde, the celebrated and now retired arthritic nude clog-dancer of Lozenge; Pierre Le Burke, itinerant emptier of cesspits and twin brothers Eugene and Latrine Thrills, retired trick cyclists, to name but a few. And so the list continued, with all of the patients interviewed, having some sort of a story to tell about a three-legged elephant called Tripod. It appeared that the staff seemed even more eccentric than the patients. But one member of staff in particular caught the interest of the great detective. He was a tall, thin and extremely well spoken Englishman whose manner and bearing (which he continually polished) were impeccable, a complete contrast to his attire that looked shabby. However, the worrying thing was the uncontrollable and frequent muffled explosions from his trouser department, that occurred whenever he moved, and which he vainly attempted to camouflage with synchronised coughing. It was also obvious to Gridlock that his face was cunningly disguised, as his nose appeared to change shape every time he coughed and glints of gold could be seen under his rather ill-fitting and obvious false teeth. Initially his manner was charming and helpful, but his demeanour changed when Gridlock informed him that he was investigating a case on behalf of Lady Bulimia Puke, who was now in residence. On hearing this, the gentleman made the excuse that it was time for him to hose down the patients and then he hurriedly ran out to the 'toilet patch' in a cloud of green vapour.

"There is something strange about that fellow," mused Gridlock.

"There's something strange about everyone here, if you ask me," answered the doctor. "But I certainly think we should keep a close watch on him. Blimey, what a terrible stench."

It had been a traumatic day for all concerned and now tired out, the two investigators decided to make their way to their rooms in order to savour their evening meal and a hot drink. As they walked down the corridor they passed Spiggott's office and could not help hearing the raised voices of Reg and Eth as they engaged in a heated argument with others in the room. Gridlock grabbed Phuckwytte's arm and signalled him to stop. The two stood outside, the doctor placing his leather ear trumpet to the door, while the detective applied his magnifying glass to one of the cracks.

"Good gracious! I can hear the sea," Phuckwytte remarked.

"Shut up you idiot!" Gridlock hissed as they eavesdropped.

"Up a bloody gum tree wivout a paddle, that's wot we are," said Reg excitedly, and interrupted by his wife saying, "A bird in the 'and is worth two up yer bush, the proof of the puddin'…"

"Yes, yes, that's all very well," said a gruff voice. "But I tell you, those two idiots are not as stupid as they look, they need to be dealt with and soon."

"I couldn't agree with you more," interjected a cultured and softly spoken reply. "These wretches must be eliminated before they find out anything."

"Mamma mia. Looka, we hav'a to draw straws."

"That's all very well," sobbed Eth, "but what about Tripod's kippers an' cigars, them's all incriminatin' evidence."

Gridlock's razor-sharp mind detected that the man Phart, the English aristocratic nurse and the height-challenged Latino were in cahoots with the Spiggotts. As they listened, Bulimia seemed to appear from nowhere and enquired what they thought they were doing. Gridlock coughed nervously and exclaimed, "There you are old chap, I told you it was a door," as he placed the magnifying glass back in his pocket.

"Yes, I agree," replied the doctor, tapping it, "and no current woodworm activity either, they must be asleep."

"Come, Lady Puke, we have much to tell you, and time is of the essence." The three of them hurried down to the detective's bedroom where an alarmed Bulimia was informed about the events that had previously taken place.

During Gridlock's report, Bulimia noticed a distinct smell of smoked herrings emanating from the pair as they sat and discussed the unresolved findings from the afternoon's interrogations that left her totally baffled. It appeared that all the staff were as much in need of mental care as the patients themselves.

"I wish we'd never come," sobbed Bulimia, "and I seem to have brought you nothing but twrouble."

"Come now, don't distress yourself," charmed Gridlock, who produced the pair of brown flannel drawers from his pocket, and offered them to dry her eyes with. Equally overcome, Phuckwytte burst into tears, blowing his nose on the nearest thing to hand which happened to be his master's carefully folded clean shirt that was lying on the bed.

"Thank you for that contribution Prunestone! I was going to wear that this evening!" remarked Gridlock angrily. "Go and blow your nose and spread your make-up on your own bloody clothes," he snarled. With that order ringing in his ears, the doctor attempted to make an excuse, but failed and shrank from the room. After an embarrassing silence Gridlock took hold of Bulimia's hand.

"Please don't worry my dearest, you're in safe hands." He moved forward and closing his eyes attempted to kiss her, but at the last moment she turned her head abruptly and his nose plunged into her ear, dislodging his monocle.

"No, no you mustn't, I'm a married woman," she admitted.

Undeterred Gridlock continued, "Oh, Bulimia, I'm completely captivated by you," and he kissed her hand.

"No, we must be careful and keep our heads," she wavered.

"I've been trying to keep mine ever since I first saw you. Please, please be mine, I love you," he announced, now on his knees. He was truly infatuated with the lady and had admitted it in no uncertain terms.

She rose in a dignified manner and replied curtly, "I'll wrespectfully see you in the morning Mr Spumes."

"And in my wildest dwreams," choked the detective as she hurriedly left his room. God! He was now even speaking like her. Love struck, rejected and knowing later that he was sure to dream of her, he tried to console himself by playing a few heart-felt passages of Paganini on his stringless violin. Even this failed to quell the passion that was now pulsing through his body. In an attempt to suppress his feelings for her, he filled his shaving bowl with cold water and immersed his wedding tackle therein. As he sat there cooling his ardour, he wondered if the lady of his longing had any idea of the agony he was now going through. Finally as a last resort, he attempted to seek comfort from his indecent magazine, turning to the centre-fold of a naked well-endowed 'Miss Bridlington' in a bending position, about to serve a shuttlecock. But her longing, come hither smile, was a poor substitute and was nothing compared with his newfound love. Thoroughly dejected, he climbed into bed and recited to himself 'I wandered lonely as a cloud' over and over again, before finally falling into a deep sleep.

Chapter 4

On the circus trail

After a dreamed night of pleasure with his newfound love, he awoke and once again found to his utmost horror that he was kissing a large bushy handlebar moustache. Phuckwytte had mistaken his master's room for the toilet in the dark, relieved himself in the wardrobe and had climbed sleepily into his bed. The rude awakening was met by a loud torrent of abuse from Gridlock and was followed by the now familiar scrotum kicking as the doctor was hastily ejected from the room.

Gridlock had now to take control of his emotions towards Lady Puke. Deep down he felt that he was fighting a losing battle, which had cost him his self-respect. He needed to get away from the chaotic surroundings and the paraphernalia and utter confusion associated with Granchez, clear his head, and concentrate on the matter in hand. While breakfast was being served, he took the liberty of asking his host if there were any local places of interest to visit, since he felt that a walk in the fresh air might be spiritually beneficial.

"Well now, let me see," pondered Reg as he scratched the stubble on his chin.

"You're too late for the Limousin cattle market," piped up Eth producing a large plate of bacon and eggs. "It were yesterday."

Undeterred, Reg continued, "There's badger baitin', owl watchin' or the snail farm up the road. Yer see the 'igh life don't start 'appenin 'till the clog dancin' in the village this evenin'." All these suggestions were met with silent indifference.

"Something a little more intellectually stimulating perhaps?" enquired the detective.

"Ah well, in that case there's the Turnip Museum in the square."

"Turnip Museum?" repeated Phuckwytte.

"They've got a much prized collection, part of the local 'istory, very interestin', even got one from the Jurassic period found in Hercule Commodes privy," said Reg, now in his element.

"Rumour 'as it that the French Revolution was started by some French peasant innocently chuckin' a rotten turnip over 'is shoulder an' cloutin' some aristocrat on the 'ead." At this point Gridlock realised that his host's intellect amounted to what was obviously on display in his beloved museum. Reg was now in full flow, giving details of what he thought was useful information.

"Then there's the tours of the Sewage Farm down river which 'ouses a vast collection of—"

"Thank you for your enlightening résumé," interrupted Gridlock.

"We'll be back for supper this evening," said Bulimia.

"'Alf past six then," Reg suggested.

"Seven it is," replied Gridlock marching out of the front door with the others in hot pursuit. Reginald Spiggott's intellect had never been exactly high in Gridlock's estimation and now, after receiving this wealth of knowledge he realised that he was dealing with a nitwit of the highest order.

It took the best part of an hour to walk into Lozenge. The only sign of life were some chickens running wild and an old woman in black herding some goats, the only vehicle being a donkey cart full of turnips driven by a toothless old man, who, as he was passing in the opposite direction, stood up, raised his cap and broke wind which they understood to be the local greeting.

The Café Filth catered for every conceivable requirement possible. It was a post office, hardware emporium, vet and brothel. This was just as well since there were no other shops at all. Apart from that, the only other relics were the church and an old pissoire in the square, around which a small group of ragged locals were playing an early form of boules with turnips and with a dead mole for the marker.

Our visitors sat down outside the café beneath its tatty awning, as the proprietor, seeing potential customers, sprang out to take their order, nodding, "Messieurs, Mesdames," while quickly brushing the remnants of a previous customer's meal off of the table and onto their laps with a dirty cloth.

The owner was a short garlic-ridden oaf with sprouting ginger hair and matching eyebrows above a ruddy wine-soaked face. His red vascular nasal protuberance had seen better days, which was more than could be said for the rest of him. He was dressed in a stained collarless striped shirt, baggy pantaloons, and clogs. A disgustingly filthy apron completed his attire. Grinning, his equally stained teeth could only be described politely in crude layman's terms as resembling a row of condemned shithouses. The man's goitred expression reminded Gridlock of a medieval gargoyle he had once seen in a cathedral on his travels. They ordered coffee and he growled something inaudible and was gone. Some minutes later, he returned with a tray of cups that emitted the delicious aroma of freshly ground coffee.

"Please excuse me gentlemen, I must visit the ladies' room," said Bulimia and left the table in search of the facility, if there was such a thing on the premises.

"So many gold-toothed characters have appeared to us," mused Gridlock as he sipped his steaming beverage. "Alf selling eel pies, Al Fred the Arab selling goat stew, Alfredo the Italian selling kipper baguettes, the hay cart driver and now the latest individual, a well spoken but flatulent Englishman. On the face of it, although gold teeth are the common link between them all, they can't all be the same person unless that person is an absolute master of disguises. And secondly," looking at Phuckwytte, "the strongman known as 'Marcel the Mangler', your baguette-stuffing admirer and the female patient Grizelda Groinstrain we both have to agree, are one and the same person."

"But how does the one legged German Von Strumphe fit into the equation, and what interests do the Spiggotts have?" Phuckwytte asked confusingly.

"And more to the point, why is our client being targeted? Is it money and position that made Lady Puke the motive?"

"That would seem to be quite obvious," came the confident reply, as moments later the lady in question returned looking even more radiant than before.

Mutual agreement resulted in them declining to experience the two recommended local historic delights, and they decided to continue with a stroll along the riverbank. It was all very pleasant during which the tranquil beauty was disturbed only by a piscatorial gentleman intent on searching for an elusive catch. The fierce midday heat caused Phuckwytte to discard his bootees, pull up his knickerbockers and to paddle in the water as his companions sat under the shade of a willow tree in silence, taking in the ambience. Gridlock watched the fisherman's occasional swish of the rod that was followed by the plop of a baited hook in the water, and an idea now formed in his mind as to how they might gain information to some unanswered questions which could help solve this case.

You have to set a sprat to catch a mackerel, thought the detective, *and in that case, why not use Prunestone as bait to extract information from this Marcel character,* a cunning master of disguise but whose real identity Gridlock, with his usual intuition and ingenuity, had uncovered. It was clear that he would have to send Prunestone to Marcel's room that very evening. Phuckwytte however, had now caught a frog that was swimming round in circles in amongst the duckweed in his bowler hat. He was like a small boy with a new toy.

"I'm going to keep it as a pet!" he said excitedly as Gridlock murmured to Bulimia that it would more likely be the other way round.

Whilst they daydreamed by the river, two bumbling ragged individuals pulling a handcart loaded with a mixture of household rubbish and scrap iron approached them. Under normal circumstances they would have been taken for tinkers, except that one was dressed as a chicken. He was short, fat and was carrying an accordion. His costume was cobbled together with an assortment of coloured scraps of material that had seen better days. The other and taller of the pair had the largest nose they had ever seen and was shaded by a moth-eaten wig, giving the appearance of a badly kept crow's nest. The clogs he was wearing had been badly adapted in an attempt to contain his huge feet by crudely sawing off the front ends, thus exposing a row of blackened hairy toes. Above him was a permanent cloud of buzzing flies and he was carrying a wooden rack full of empty bottles that completed this strange combination. They stopped and introduced themselves by executing a series of cartwheels, after which they bowed and applauded themselves. It transpired that they were house clearing at present, but were in fact travelling musicians connected to a circus in the area. Their job as Barkers was to drum up an audience for the 'Big Top' as they called it. At that moment, as if by magic, they fell into a vigorous song and dance routine that astounded the onlookers. The 'chicken' played his accordion which, due to an unfortunate split in the bellows, just gave off a wheezing moan, whilst the 'nose' had more success as he engaged his cavernous nostrils in order to blow and sniff into the empty bottles, which emitted a strange honking sound not unlike tuneless Peruvian pan pipes. As their act reached a loud crescendo, the 'nose' sneezed, projecting his ill fitting dentures past Bulimia's shoulder, and embedding them into the tree under which they were sitting.

"I say, these 'Johnny Foreigners' certainly know how to entertain," said Phuckwytte excitedly.

Hmm, not exactly chamber music from the Café Royal, thought Gridlock unimpressed. The 'nose' extracted his false teeth, wiped them on his sleeve, replaced them and retrieved his cap and held it out in the hope of receiving some sort of reward. Gridlock on the other hand, politely asked him to take his 'chicken' companion, the cart and his flies away with him.

After the two performers had disappeared, the detective asked, "I suppose you didn't notice the distinctively colourful poster on the back of the handcart did you?"

"No," confessed the others.

"Well, while you were being entertained by those performing fools I made a note of it." He produced his pocket notepad and read: "Luigi Vaselino's Circus. See performing live trapeze artists, fire eaters etc, etc... Here's the important bit. See 'The Great Castrato', hypnotist, illusionist and mind-reader.' The very same advertised on the back of your blackmail note my dear."

"Oh Gridlock, you're wonderful," Bulimia said, as she gave the detective a warm and forgiving hug.

It was now late; the sun had set low on the horizon, and it was time for them to head back to Granchez. Phuckwytte absentmindedly donned his hat, and was showered by a cascade of stinking river water.

"Oh dear, you seem to have lost your newfound pet," Gridlock mused. "About time you had a wash," he remarked.

His companion made no comment, but sulked child-like for the rest of the journey back to Granchez. Gridlock had impressed Bulimia with his calculated and quick observation, and it was evident that she was pleased. Now, in high spirits, he chatted and laughed with her all the way back. After a considerable time they entered the lane leading down to their lodgings. They were now exhausted after their eventful day and the journey back, but Gridlock was still planning ahead.

"We must try and find out exactly where and when this foreign 'eyetie' circus is performing, infiltrate it and question this Castrato fellow. I'm sure he's implicated." It was some time before Phuckwytte finally spoke.

"I know where it is and when it starts," he grudgingly admitted.

"I suppose you're now going to tell us you're psychic," teased Gridlock. Phuckwytte produced a screwed up piece of paper from his pocket.

"It says so here," he pointed to the flyer he'd been given.

"Where did you get this from?" snorted Gridlock.

"The 'chicken' man gave it to me," he answered meekly.

Furious, Gridlock shouted, "Why in God's teeth man didn't you tell us you had this information?"

"You never asked me," came the mild response.

Gridlock thought to himself and considered, *the sooner I use Phuckwytte as bait to try and solve this case the better.* There was a message from home waiting for him on the hall table from Lilly, which read: 'Annual subscription to the Cavendish Club has lapsed. Colonel Carruthers called. Letter from Cox & Co Bank arrived. Weather's foul. Sputum sends his love.'

"Sparse, but straight and to the point as usual," he remarked, climbing upstairs to change. It was then he remembered that he would now have to wear his only spare shirt, the front of which Phuckwytte had so thoughtlessly used as a handkerchief. To hide this embarrassment, he tucked his spare pair of long johns down the front of his evening dress, knowing this probably wouldn't be noticed by his fashion conscious hosts.

Chapter 5

As the plot quickens, thickens and sickens

Night had fallen and the grandfather clock in the hall downstairs struck midnight, then one and two in that order, as the two men still argued over Gridlock's proposed plan of sending the hapless doctor (dressed in a flimsy seductive negligee), to glean and extract information from the circus strongman.

"That monster frightens me, there's something not quite right about him. Why don't you go yourself if you think he knows so much? Why the hell pick me?" queried the doctor.

"Tush, tush, don't irk yourself so. The fact is that the man has, shall we say... a fascination for your charms. You will be in no danger, I assure you, and should he become overzealous, I'm quite sure that you, dear doctor, will be able to handle the situation with ease. Just keep calm and extract as much information as you can from him." Prunestone reluctantly relented and prepared himself for the assignation. The detective praised Phuckwytte's courage and tenacity, but inwardly he was smiling, for only he, Gridlock Spumes, had now formulated an idea as to who the real identity of the mysterious person from his past was.

Should I reveal my predication to Prunestone? he thought. *No, why spoil such a splendid game. He will find out himself soon enough!*

Prunestone left his quarters in darkness and proceeded to tiptoe down the seemingly endless corridor towards the Mangler's room, colliding with the unforgiving stone-clad walls as he went, and cursing to himself for not having lit his candle. Fumbling around in his handbag, he eventually found some matches and lit it, (his candle not his handbag).

What a silly me, he thought to himself, nearly setting light to his wig. Throughout the house, doors were now being slammed, bolted and locked. Gradually the silence gave way to the sound of whimpering, moaning and cries, which slowly rose to a crescendo of curses, shouts, wailing and maniacal laughter. Stopping for a moment, he listened to the cacophony of sounds and said to himself: *Reminds me of lights out in the dorm at my old prep school. Those were the days!*

Adjusting his bustle he moved forward scrutinising the numbers on each bedroom door. He was putting on a brave face behind the make-up, for although he had always been loyal and devoted to his colleague, on this occasion he felt a little too much was being asked of him. Outwardly he tried to appear calm, but inside his stomach was churning. For although he had been a blatant cross-dresser since childhood, the very thought of flirting with the oaf he was about to meet, in an attempt to gain information, appalled him. However, he had been cajoled by Gridlock, and was quietly confident that his most seductive clothing, wig and perfume would knock the strongman off his feet, so to speak. Holding the candle up to a rough wooden door on which the number 69 was crudely chalked, he thought, *Ah! Soixante-neuf, this is the one,* and knocked six times as agreed.

The door was unbolted, and a huge and heavily tattooed arm plucked the frightened doctor off his feet, and threw him onto the straw mattress in the corner of the room. Marcel, who was still adorned in his golden locks and hopsack dress, threw himself onto the bed next to the now terrified doctor, uttering words of love and devotion. After much struggling, the petrified Phuckwytte hastily scrambled to his feet, toyed with his wig and backed gingerly away remarking, "How fetching the curtains and rugs are. What a delightful décor and a marvellous array of candles... how tasteful."

"I did it for you ma leetle one. I wanted zis occasion to be trez romantique." The strongman moved behind the nervous visitor and rested his great hands upon his shoulders. A fine picture they made, silhouetted against a background of flickering candlelight, the 'Mangler' with his waist-length golden locks, broken nose and unshaved chin, with one shoulder strap falling carelessly over his hairy arm, and the sackcloth dress finally resting in crumpled folds on his two great mud-caked boots. Phuckwytte was now perspiring heavily. His breathing became erratic, and he was visibly trembling.

Why have I allowed myself to go along with this idiotic charade? he thought.

Information, information! Just pull yourself together man and get on with it, he said to himself as he moved away quickly from his amorous captor, who was now attempting to stroke his knee.

"How dare you," he uttered, while retrieving a small fan from his handbag, which he began to wave frantically in front of his crimson face. Moving to the armchair, he sat down and demanded, "I'll have you know that I'm a virgin, a gentleman physician and above all, a former officer in the Queen's army, and as such, I insist on being treated as one."

"Yes, yes, of course ma leetle one," replied Marcel, falling to his knees and clasping the doctor's hands.

"Pleeze forgive me for my naughty behaviour and tell me zat we can still remain friends." Hearing this, Phuckwytte became more confident.

"If you care for me as much as you say, of course, but only on one condition. First, I need details from you," he said sitting back, crossing his legs, unknowingly revealing his lace knickers. "I believe you have certain facts concerning 'The Great Castrato' and his cronies. If that is the case, I want you to let me know all you can about them." The strongman's face changed and drained of colour, as he seriously considered his position.

"Very well," he mumbled, "but only for you would I do such a thing, for I am sworn to secrecy."

Phuckwytte listened intently to the Mangler's story, occasionally taking notes in his little pink notebook, and by the time the clock struck six thirty-two, he had written all he could. Making his excuses he left, retracing his steps down the corridor as the love-struck hulk blew him kisses.

As dawn was breaking into a thousand pieces, he opened the door to his master's room. Gridlock was already up and dressed, sitting with his back to the door and staring out of the window. He was swathed in clouds of tobacco smoke, and between puffs of his pipe, he stuffed a handful of liquorice allsorts into his mouth. The doctor had observed the super sleuth in this mood before and the signs were not good. With this in mind, he closed the door quietly behind him and politely coughed. Hearing this, the detective swung round on the ornate piano stool, which swivelled to its highest adjustment, causing the seat to spin off the pillar, along with its occupant, who hit his head on the edge of the sink. He rose slowly and fixed Phuckwytte with a piercing stare.

"Well Prunestone?" he blurted, forgetting that his mouth was still full of the black sticky substance, which now projected itself at Phuckwytte's sweaty face.

"Well, what?" demanded the doctor. "Just look at me! I suppose you would now like me to sing something from the Swanny Minstrel Show?" He then grabbed Gridlock's favourite deerstalker from the hat stand and wiped the black goo from his saturated countenance. "I see you are at that evil confectionary again Gridlock. I strongly advise you to wean yourself back onto sherbet lemons or face the consequences."

"And what consequences are those pray?"

"I don't know, but I'll ruddy well think of some," replied the annoyed doctor.

"Balderdash and piffle," retorted Gridlock rubbing the distinctive lump that was now appearing on his forehead. "When a great mind such as mine is challenged, it needs sustenance. But more to the point, how did you fare with the 'Mangler'? Did your visit bear fruit?"

"Well, we did partake of some rather fine cherry cake, which we washed down with some delightful lemon cordial."

"Prunestone dear fellow, sarcasm has never been your strongest asset, and I sometimes wonder if your staircase actually reaches the top floor. Was the man forthcoming with information?"

"As a matter of fact, he was too bloody forthcoming," the doctor replied petulantly. "And may I also take this opportunity in thanking you for showing your usual regard for my welfare."

Gridlock's manner immediately changed. "Now, now, Prunestone old chap," replied the seemingly concerned detective. "Of course I had no fears whatsoever for your safety. Not you, my dear friend – a man of your calibre; a man of your infinite courage and determination. Here, have a sup of brandy and tell me all," said Gridlock producing his hipflask.

Prunestone took a large gulp and commenced to impart all that he had discovered. When he had finished, Gridlock threw his arms round his surprised manservant and exclaimed, "Phuckwytte, you truly are the salt of the earth. To tell you the truth, I had begun to despair with this case, but now everything seems to be falling into place. Hurrah for you Phuckwytte! Hurrah again I say. Let's drink to the success of the venture." By now Phuckwytte was quite tipsy.

"Old habits die hard, eh, Gridlock old man," slurred the half-inebriated doctor. "May I join you?" and with that, the two men hopped frantically around the room in delirious abandon.

"Have another swig old bean."

"I say Spumes," confessed the doctor, "I used to have a drink problem, but now I love the stuff!" With that, they both collapsed in hysterical laughter. This prompted Gridlock to crouch down to half his height and begin to hop backwards and forwards across the room on one leg – the result of undergoing severe torture whilst serving in the British Army. Whenever he felt close to solving a case, he would do the crouching, one-legged hop for hours on end.

"Old habits die hard, eh, Gridlock old man," slurred the half-inebriated doctor. "May I join you?" and with that, the two men hopped frantically around the room in delirious abandon.

So ecstatic were the two that they failed to notice the incredulous expressions on the faces of the Spiggotts outside, as they pressed their noses to the grimy window and peered into the room. This was strange, since Gridlock's room was on the first floor and ten foot above the ground. The patrons of Granchez had seen and heard enough. They fell into the garden in a heap. Panic-stricken, they hitched their old nag up to the cart and made their way to Vaselino's Big Top, for they needed to impart what had been seen and heard, to their mysterious master. Spumes and Prunestone were now exhausted, and collapsed breathlessly to the floor, unable to continue with their strange ritual any longer. Some moments later Gridlock heard a tap on his door.

"See who it is," he ordered. Phuckwytte obliged, only to discover a tatty envelope that had been pushed under it.

"What's that?" enquired Gridlock.

"It's a flier, same as the last one, advertising the whereabouts of Vaselino's Circus, which has apparently just opened in a field on the outskirts of Lozenge. There's also a handwritten note. Hang on, I'll read it: 'The Great Castrato', hypnotist and mind reader extraordinaire, invites you to meet him at his caravan at six thirty sharp this evening'. Great heavens, how extraordinary," muttered the doctor.

"Well Prunestone, we had better get changed as this is one invitation we cannot afford to turn down. Of course, it could be a trap so we had better take precautions. Place my trusty wooden truncheon somewhere under your petticoat, while I shall make use of my Amazonian blowpipe and a handful of darts. Their tips are already dipped in a solution of lark's vomit and Dr Silas Minger's famous seedpod remedy. It never fails. Once infected with this mixture, any would-be assailant will be left in a coma for hours with immediate effect!"

That evening, thus equipped, the two men followed the instructions and made their way on foot to Vaselino's Circus, eager, but at the same time apprehensive, of their forthcoming rendezvous. As they approached the perimeter of the circus with its assortment of caravans, tents and cages, they were greeted by a group of tumbling dwarfs, jugglers and acrobats.

"Come with us," said one. "You are expected."

The circus artists continued to tumble their way ahead and were joined by a raggle-taggle of various other entertainers, including a bearded lady, an assortment of clowns, trapeze artists and freaks of every description. There was even a top-hatted gentleman walking on stilts. The entertainers hesitated and began to murmur amongst themselves as they approached a large garishly painted caravan. Phuckwytte pointed to a writhing man in a cage, who was covered in chains, padlocks, handcuffs and leg irons. He was struggling violently to get free.

"Who on earth is that?" enquired the doctor. "And why is he bound up so?"

"Oh, 'im," replied one of the dwarfs. "That's Geraldo Fig our escapologist, 'e used to bite the 'eads off live pigeons!"

"Good grief!" exclaimed the doctor appalled at the prospect, as the little man continued.

"Just tryin' out his new act, but it ain't worked so far. Three weeks now 'ees bin in there."

"Can't somebody find the keys and help the poor wretch?" asked Phuckwytte.

At this, the strange assembly burst into fits of laughter as the bearded lady explained, "Well, the actual truth is, we're forbidden to help 'im."

"Oh?"

"He's in the Master's bad books, 'avin' eaten one of the performin' penguins!"

The caravan door was opened by 'The Elastic Man', whose loose skin hung about his body like a curtain, and who announced, "'The Great Castrato' will see you now." The pair peered into the gloomy interior and as their eyes grew accustomed to the dark, a luminous white-gloved hand appeared and beckoned them to enter.

"Be seated," the owner of the hand commanded, in a deep and resonant voice, which seemed to come from a faceless hooded figure at the far end of the unlit caravan. Phuckwytte did so immediately, but Gridlock remained standing and said he preferred to converse on his feet. Barely visible in the gloomy interior, were two other strange looking creatures, squatting on the floor each side of the hooded figure.

"Good Lord," whispered Phuckwytte. "It's those two fellows we met on the road the other day, one dressed as a chicken and the other with a huge nose and ill-fitting wig."

The faceless one spoke. "So, Gridlock Spumes, the great detective and his witless and effeminate colleague, Phuckwytte Prunestone. I'm delighted to make your acquaintance."

"How dare you call me witless. I'll have you know that I have served as a doctor in the British Army," blurted out Phuckwytte.

"The Queen's own regiment no doubt," replied the voice, at which time the 'chicken' and 'nose' collapsed into laughter.

"Why, you cowardly blaggard," cried the doctor. "Stop hiding in the shadows and face me like a man," he demanded.

"Calm yourself Prunestone, don't rise to his cheap quips," said Gridlock. "My colleague is right. I demand that you show yourself sir, this instant, and make it clear why we have been summoned. For I, too, have some questions to put to you."

"All in good time, gentlemen, but you will forgive me if I remain hidden for the present. However I'm delighted to converse with the famous Spumes, a man who possesses an intellect almost as great as my own. Whose razor-sharp mind and powers of observation have solved some of the most baffling crimes of the century. A man, who at present is worthy to pit his wits against myself, 'The Great Castrato'. A pseudonym, of course, but one which is known throughout the length of Europe. However, unlike yourself, I am a master of disguise. But please, forgive me, what a careless host I am. Would you care for some refreshment?" He passed a silver tray to the 'chicken' who rose and offered it on to the pair. Gridlock examined the two glasses of Vimto and the bowl of black and coloured confectionary.

"You see, Mr Spumes, I'm already aware of your addiction."

Gridlock observed the liquorice with his magnifying glass and then took one of the sweets, tasted it and spat it out. "So, you think you can fool me with cheap foreign imports? Think again Castrato," and he thrust the tray back to the 'chicken', who began to devour them greedily.

"You're correct, of course, Mr Spumes. However, the flavour does improve with age, and you like them, don't you, 'Broody'?" He then patted the 'chicken' on the head as its owner started making loud clucking noises.

Gridlock surveyed his enemy. "So you are 'The Great Castrato', the man who dares not to show his face and who hides under a false name."

"Prepare yourself, Spumes," answered Castrato, "for I am about to reveal my true identity. It matters not if you know now, because neither of you will live long enough to pass on the information. I am none other than the twin brother of your archenemy Professor Biryani, the man you had arrested last year, who was unfairly tried and incarcerated in the Tower of London for so-called crimes against humanity. You remain silent Spumes; is this little surprise too much for you to digest? Shall I go further?" Castrato continued unabated.

"I have been my brother's partner in crime for years and together we were responsible for the attempted theft of the Crown Jewels and the successful 'Great Bank of England' robbery. Our confidence and daring knows no bounds. We sold the Eiffel Tower twice, London Bridge three times and we are currently involved in a sale to the Americans of the little eel, pie and mash stall on the corner of East Street Market in Southwark!" While Castrato was raving on, Gridlock casually turned his back to the power-crazed lunatic, slowly removed the pre-loaded blowpipe from his inside jacket, and swiftly putting it to his mouth, turned and aimed towards the figure and blew.

"Aaaaaaaaagh!" cried Castrato. "You swine Spumes, what have you done?" This question was terminated as the dart swiftly did its work. As quick as a flash, Gridlock reloaded and fired two more, as the 'chicken' and 'nose' rose to defend their master, but surprise combined with accuracy was on the detective's side, and they froze like statues.

Outside, the caravan was now surrounded by a screaming mob of circus folk loyal to their leader.

"Right, Prunestone old man, looks like we have to make a dash for it. No other way."

The doctor hitched up his skirt and withdrew his truncheon. "I'm ready for the blighters," he said.

Gridlock grabbed a heavy soup ladle hanging from the ceiling of the van and shouted, "Now!" and he kicked open the door, making short work of the clowns and dwarfs who tried to block their passage. These were then replaced by a howling mob of fire-eaters, knife throwers and other performers. A sharp blow from Phuckwytte's truncheon felled the bearded lady, while the rest fled in horror, as he threatened to lift his skirt and expose himself. Geraldo Fig was left still struggling in his chains. The man on stilts was now approaching at a rapid pace, cursing and shouting obscenities. Phuckwytte and Gridlock threw themselves at the two stilts and proceeded to rock them to and fro, until the performer finally lost his balance, and fell like a mighty oak, into the circus animals' great steaming heap of manure.

Having escaped by the skin of their pules, our triumphant pair sped towards Granchez as fast as their legs would carry them. Out of breath, they turned only briefly to catch a glimpse of the havoc they had caused. When they finally arrived at Granchez, the men made straight for Bulimia's room to report their findings, but were shocked to find it empty of all her belongings, as even her cherished chamber pot had gone. Gridlock looked around in disbelief, and his eyes alighted on the wax-sealed envelope addressed to him. On opening it, the contents read: 'Dearest Gridlock, I'm afraid that our relationship must come to an end forthwith, as my husband Lord Methane has got wind, (so to speak) of our liaison. I fear the consequences could be calamitous for both of us. Please try not to think too badly of me my dear, I will always cherish the time we spent together. Ever yours, Bulimia.'

"Curses and damnation," cried the wounded sleuth. "The only woman in my life I have truly loved and now she has left me. Oh, what an unhappy wretch I am!"

"She obviously intended to leave the letter in your room, but thought better of it," the doctor perceived. With that Gridlock sloped off to his accommodation, followed by his concerned companion. Taking up his string-less violin, he now launched into playing music so melancholic that the doctor was reduced to floods of tears. After Gridlock had returned the violin to its case, Phuckwytte shoved a handful of fresh liquorice into Gridlock's mouth, lit his pipe, handed it to him and then retired sadly back to his own room.

The following day, Phuckwytte purloined a clean shirt from one of the inmates to replace his masters, in an attempt to make amends. However, to Gridlock's dismay when he tried the garment on, it reached the floor and had three sleeves. Having now regained his composure after three pipes of tobacco, he raised himself from the armchair and cried out with a mad euphoric look of inspiration.

"I have it Prunestone, yes! I have it, by God, I have it!"

"Not contagious is it? Where does it hurt? Do you wish me to examine you?"

"Silence you idiot and listen."

"I can't hear anything?"

"I haven't said it yet, you buffoon," exploded Gridlock, making a mental note to throttle Phuckwytte at the earliest opportunity.

"We are indeed fighting a ruthless and cunning foe, but Castrato has underestimated my formidable powers of detection. With the information you gleaned from your admirer, the 'Mangler', combined with what I discovered hidden in the stable during my early morning stroll, I'm sure that we will soon have our quarry trapped. But dear boy, I'll need your help to present the evidence and prove our case. Arrange immediately for the Spiggotts, their staff, the patients, Marcel, Von Strumphe and the less dangerous inmates, to meet us in the barn within the next thirty minutes. Tell them that I need to see them all as a matter of great urgency."

Half an hour later, the strange assortment of guests duly made their way to the barn and took their chairs, which had been arranged in a semi-circle around a pile of straw bales, upon which the great detective stood, centre stage. When all had settled down, an agitated Reg stood up and asked what it was all about.

"I 'ope it's important 'cos we got the bedpans to empty, ain't we Eth?"

"Yes we 'ave," she replied.

"I believe you will find what I have to say most interesting," announced Gridlock. "I will endeavour not to keep you too long, for I know how pressing your duties are. Firstly, I would like to deal with our mysterious cigar-smoking, piano-playing elephant, Tripod." At the mention of the name, a hush descended as the audience froze in terror.

"Rest assured," he continued, "there is no such thing as this piano-playing, three-legged animal. He is a myth, a creation, invented by the Spiggotts to keep patients in a continual state of fear."

"It's a lie!" screamed Ethel Spiggott, springing to her feet.

"It's a bleedin' lie, 'ow dare you accuse my Reg and me of such a wicked thing."

"Please sit down, Mrs Spiggott and calm yourself. Now would my assistant Doctor Prunestone, with the help of your staff, please bring forth the evidence?" The two great barn doors were opened as the doctor and designated helpers wheeled in a life-size model of a three-legged elephant. There was a sigh of amazement from the assembled patients, as the effigy was pushed along, groaning and squeaking towards the centre.

"This is nothing but a papier-mâché life-size model, cunningly designed, constructed and painted by Herr Shortarshe Von Strumphe," he said pointing at the accused. There was a hushed whispering and nodding of heads from the spectators.

"Stand up and come to me at once," ordered Gridlock. Von Strumphe stood up nervously and hopped on his leg towards the detective.

"Nein, nein, zey made me do it!" cried Von Strumphe, falling on his one knee and grovelling on the floor. "Zey threatened to reveal zer secrets of my musical hairpieces to zer hairdressers and vigmaker's guild if I did not carry out zeir orders. It vould haf shpelt ruin for me, my vife und all zer leeltle Strumphe's, please haf mercy on me." This admission was met with some scepticism.

"Nevertheless, Von Strumphe, you've been hoisted with your own petard."

"Zat is not zo. I haf no such thing about mine person!" protested the little German.

"Please return to your seat and I'll deal with you later," ordered Gridlock harshly, as the whimpering accused was helped back to his seat.

At this point the Spiggotts were attempting to make their escape as they slowly backed up towards the open doors.

"Stay where you are!" cried Phuckwytte, in his most authoritative voice. Reg and Eth froze, and then shuffled back to their places.

Now standing on the makeshift straw podium, Gridlock adopted the attitude of a prosecuting barrister in full flow. Looking down at the Spiggots, he announced, "Do you two miserable miscreants deny that you blackmailed the unfortunate Strumphe into constructing Tripod, with the aim of putting the fear of God into the hearts of everyone at Granchez?" The couple shook their bowed heads.

"Do you acknowledge the fact that you've been running this disgusting and bogus establishment, under the direction of the so-called 'Great Castrato' and his henchmen?" The Spiggotts nodded.

"I further accuse you of advertising this sham of a rest home with promises of luxury, comfort, the best medical attention and tender loving care. That when your affluent guests arrive, they're sedated and incarcerated in this revolting and unsanitary asylum, where they are systematically robbed of all their worldly goods, and then held for ransom to their wealthy families. Adding insult to injury, that they are kept in a state of semi-consciousness and fed the most disgusting filth, that you refer to as food."

"I object!" screamed Eth. "We've 'ad no complaints. My food is not disgustin' filth, is it Reg?"

"No, not always," replied her husband forlornly. But Gridlock continued unabated.

"And that you continue to hold your hapless captives in these unspeakable conditions until a ransom has been paid to release them, and if the money is not forthcoming within a certain time, they mysteriously disappear without trace?" The spectators were now completely dumbstruck, for none of them had any idea as to what the Spiggotts had been up to.

"Have you anything to say in your defence?" asked Phuckwytte.

"Yes, I 'ave," replied Reg, wiping the beads of sweat which were now pouring down his face. "We was forced into wot we done, after runnin' an honest Chambre D'hotes 'ere wiv all mod cons. We gave good value for money, until he arrived wiv his gang of villains, and threatened us wiv closure and bankruptcy unless we complied wiv his evil plans."

"Who do you mean by 'he' exactly?" enquired Gridlock.

"That bleedin' Castrato, of course," sobbed Eth. "He's the mastermind behind everyfink. He's evil, I tell you, pure evil."

"We ain't the only ones," interrupted Reg. "Why, the wicked scoundrel has a network of rest 'omes, all doin' the same thing. Now it's out in the open, I hope he rots in 'ell," he confessed.

"This 'ere Vaselino's Circus is just a front. He travels all round France wiv it, collectin' his ill-gotten gains."

Gridlock ignored the pleading and began his summing up.

"It's the two of you we're dealing with at the moment. Your personal involvement with these heinous crimes will be dealt with, all in good time, and leniency may be considered towards you, because of your repentance and cooperation. But finally, I have one question to ask. In front of all these good people gathered here, please tell us the true identity of 'The Great Castrato'." Reg looked around furtively at the assembled crowd, and began to relinquish his information.

"The true identity of 'The Great Castrato' is... aaaaaargh," Spiggott's sentence was cut short by a tall, well-spoken member of staff, standing immediately next him. The man had raised his right leg and emitted a silent sulphurous cloud from his posterior that enshrouded the couple.

"Corr... pheww... aaagh!" They choked as he leapt to one side, lit a match and threw it in their direction and bolted for the door. The naked flame ignited the gas, rendering the couple even more senseless than normal, by the ensuing explosion.

'Marcel the Mangler' anticipated the attempted escape and stuck his foot out, sending the would-be assassin sprawling.

"Apprehend that man," the 'Mangler' ordered, throwing off his golden locks, hopsack dress and French accent. Now, clad only in his long johns and hobnailed boots he announced, "I am Inspector Todger of Scotland Yard, known to my friends and colleagues as 'Knackers of the Yard'."

"So we can all see," the shocked Phuckwytte remarked, studying Todger's protuberance in his close fitting long johns.

"I hereby arrest you for the attempted murder of Mr and Mrs Spiggott and anything you may say will be taken down and used as evidence against you."

"Trousers," a patient at the back shouted, and was knocked unconscious.

"Sergeant and constable, handcuff that man," Todger ordered his two incognito policemen. "We have been following you for some time, and I am delighted to say we now have you, the so-called 'Great Castrato'. At last in our custody!" At this, Gridlock announced that the inspector had indeed arrested a major player in this game, but that the felon, however, standing before them, was not in fact Castrato.

"The mastermind behind these unspeakable crimes is none other than…" but before Spumes could finish his sentence, the doors at both ends of the barn crashed open and issued forth a horde of Castrato's gang members, still dressed in their circus costumes. They quickly surrounded the assembled guests in a menacing fashion.

The last person to enter the barn was an elegantly dressed figure in a ringmaster's outfit, who commanded, "Stop!" The figure wore a red frockcoat, black top hat, riding boots, white jodhpurs, waistcoat, and sported a huge drooping handlebar moustache. A long bullwhip was clasped in their white-gloved hand.

"Bulimia!" exclaimed a shocked and almost apoplectic Prunestone. For he had recognised at once the voice and shapely figure of their female adversary.

"Lady Bulimia Puke to you… you bumbling and pathetic cross-dresser. Yes, it is I, 'The Great Castrato'. Release my husband, you inept simpletons," she shouted. She then cracked her whip and screamed, as it caught the tip of her right ear.

"With pleasure," replied the inspector coughing, and holding his nose against the stench. Methane now sprang to where his wife stood, followed by a further series of resonant anal retorts. Lady Puke embraced her husband triumphantly and continued to taunt her enemies.

"Pray tell me Spumes, how does it feel to be defeated and jilted by a woman? Confess to me you had no idea that it was I who posed as 'The Great Castrato'!" The detective was now completely bewildered but tried to keep his nerve.

"Your voice did have me fooled, but you need not have tried to convince me that you had a twin brother. For you have exactly the same abnormalities as Professor Biryani, my archenemy. I refer of course to the unnatural third nipple, and to the heart-shaped mole on your left buttock, a birth mark you both share!" At this revelation, Lord Methane became most upset.

"God's teeth! Is nothing sacred? You swine, Spumes, she's my wife. I'll shoot you down like a dog! Please tell me it's not true," he ranted, turning to his spouse. "Tell me that this poltroon has not defiled you, my own true love, my reason for being."

"For being what?" came the reply. "Now, now, who's a jealous little Methane?" she teased, stroking his chin with her whip.

"A man has to do what a man has to do, and a girl has to chew what a girl has to chew!" With that, she cracked her whip again and ordered her thugs at the top of her voice, "Take no prisoners!" All hell broke loose as the circus folk closed in on those assembled; deafening cries of terror arose as the more dangerous inmates charged into the melée. The uproar in the barn had reached their ears, some of it had reached their noses, but whatever it reached, they wanted blood.

Chapter 6

The hunters are being hunted

Our two captured heroes were now in great danger at the hands, knees and teeth of a woman who would stop at nothing now that her identity had been exposed. The knowledge, now in their possession, could result with their elimination, or worse still, their being press-ganged into joining the circus. During the violent confrontation the pair had been overcome, bound and thrown down into an old wine cellar, where they considered their fate. The crestfallen Gridlock was heartbroken and at the same time angry with himself, for falling in love had clouded his judgement and he had committed the cardinal sin of becoming emotionally involved with his client. The whole business had been a farce. He had been duped into investigating a fabricated crime in order to get him out of England – but why? The reason still remained a mystery. Apart from that, Bulimia had lied to him all along. Her husband had not been shooting with her father back in Selsey, England, but was already here when she arrived. The ransom letter she had written to herself, the illiterate handwritten messages on circus programmes were lies, lies, all lies. The detective had been humiliated, shamed, tricked and hoodwinked and had lost badly in the game of love.

Phuckwytte on the other hand, remained in a black mood. During the affray, his coiffure and attire had suffered considerable damage. The sleeve of his blouse had been torn off along with his pearl necklace, and one false eyelash had gone missing.

"I've split a nail," he complained. "I knew I should have worn gloves," he whimpered.

"Oh shut up for Christ's sake, I'm trying to think," snapped Gridlock.

"And not only that, I've laddered my best pair of silk stockings," Phuckwytte sighed.

"That's the least of our blasted problems!" snarled the irritated detective as he surveyed their surroundings.

After some time, Phuckwytte was feeling a little more cheerful and quipped, "Cheer up old chap, it could be worse. At least we're alive and in one piece."

Gridlock was now suffering severe withdrawal symptoms, for it had been some time since he had run out of his supply of precious liquorice, and he was in no mood for small talk.

"That's very good of you to say so Prunestone, under the circumstances," he shouted.

"Well I was only trying to be helpful," admitted the doctor.

"Helpful! Helpful! You're not at all bloody helpful!" yelled Gridlock, enraged. Phuckwytte as usual, burst into tears which inevitably happened when he was shouted at. The cellar was dark and damp and it exuded a prevailing smell of stale wine, the musty odour being reminiscent of the seedier kind of East End gin palaces found between Bermondsey and Deptford Reach.

117

Above the doctor's complaints of being unable to retrieve his lace handkerchief, due to the fact that his hands were tied behind his back, Gridlock heard another sound coming from inside a huge wooden wine vat in the corner.

"Hush Prunestone!" he commanded. "It seems that we are not entirely alone in this God-forsaken place." Sounds of snoring accompanied by the occasional postern blast were heard echoing around the container.

"Hello, is anybody in?" enquired Gridlock.

"Cooee," Phuckwytte joined in.

"I say you, you in there, identify yourself," Gridlock ordered. With that, the unseen occupant belched loudly and began to sing the Marseillaise.

"The man's drunk!" remarked Phuckwytte.

"That is an understatement. I dare say you'd be somewhat inebriated sleeping in an empty wine vat, the fumes alone would knock you out. I wonder how much of the contents he has sampled," surmised the detective and tried again.

"Ahoy there, anyone in?"

"Pardonnez Monsieur?"

"To whom do I have the pleasure of addressing?" asked Gridlock.

"It is I. Pierre," replied the drunken voice.

"What are you doing in there?"

"I'm not doing anything in here!" replied the indignant Frenchman.

"We urgently need your assistance, could you please climb out and set us free," they begged. After several unsuccessful attempts the man finally extracted himself from his sleeping place, staggered to his feet, raised his moth-eaten cap from above a nose which looked more like a bloodshot cauliflower, bowed low and introduced himself.

"I am Pierre Le Burke, the local emptier of cesspits," he announced, offering a filthy, stained hand, which due to their predicament fortunately could not be shaken. "Known locally as 'Visage de Merde'."

"Pardon?"

"'Shit face'," he proudly proclaimed. At this introduction, the bound captives were unable to take evasive action in order to hold their noses. Gridlock responded as he tried to unsuccessfully position himself upwind.

"Would you please be kind enough to untie us this instant?"

"It would be most favourable under the circumstances," piped up the doctor.

"Certainly," replied 'Shit face' as he tried to focus on this task, lost his balance, fell backwards onto the littered debris that covered the cellar floor, and passed out.

"Splendid! Now what the bloody hell are we going to do?" said Gridlock.

"Well, we'll just have to wait until he regains consciousness, which judging by the state of him, could be ages," observed Phuckwytte. "I suppose we could play I-Spy to pass the time."

This suggestion was met by a stony silence, as the frustrated pair just waited without speaking. The doctor, however, was right in his estimation, for it was some hours, during which they were subjected to the Frenchman's nocturnal and pungent seismic eruptions, before he finally came round and enquired, "Who are you?"

Our heroes then re-introduced themselves, and explained the dangerous position they were in. All this was news to our pungent alcoholic, for he couldn't remember anything, but being convinced of their plight, he clumsily attempted to release the pair.

As dawn slowly began to break it was accompanied by the usual crescendo of French birdsong, (some of them also sang in English and the odd one or two in Arabic). Our two stalwarts quietly collected their belongings and along with their smelly accomplice, made a hasty escape into the welcomed farmyard air.

"Shouldn't we have left the Spiggotts a thank you note?" asked Phuckwytte.

"What have we got to thank them for? It hasn't been a particularly pleasant stay. In any case, once they realise we've gone and are on the run, the whole mob will be searching for us. We must get to the village, assess the situation and plan our next move." They set out and were again met by the same toothless old man driving his turnip laden donkey cart, who offered them the same informal greeting as before, only louder.

They finally reached the village, but had to wait some time before the Café Filth was opened. The patron resplendent in a rat-gnawed striped nightshirt, took their order for coffee and croissants, nodded obligingly, and disappeared into the back room. Over a hearty breakfast discussion, they concluded that some form of disguise would be advisable in order to avoid capture. Gridlock instructed Phuckwytte to 'borrow' some French clothing from neighbouring washing lines.

"I will remain here and guard our possessions," he suggested and proceeded to order more coffee and croissants for himself. Phuckwytte eventually arrived back with a bundle of clothing under his arm.

"What in God's name is this?" Gridlock exclaimed in horror, holding up a complete nun's outfit.

"It's all I could find," pleaded the doctor.

"So what are you going to wear then?"

"My best day dress," replied Phuckwytte sheepishly.

"Now listen here. Happily I don't share the same passion for women's clothing as you do Prunestone, but is there no male attire to be had?"

"No one will ever recognize you in that costume Monsieur," added 'Shit face' suppressing a snigger. They paid their bill and crossed the square to the old pissoire to change and create their deception. Gridlock was the first to enter.

"Mind where you stand Monsieur," advised 'Shit face'.

"If anyone finds out about this back in London, I'll be the laughing stock of the Carlton Club," Gridlock moaned. Finally he appeared from behind the metal screen.

"Well… how do I look?" he enquired. Phuckwytte scrutinised his master.

"Hmm… try padding yourself in the appropriate places with some of your underwear," he suggested. "Your right breast appears to be a little bigger and more lopsided than the left… Ah, that's better, up a little more… that'll have to do. One thing though, you still haven't mastered the correct stance that one would expect of a Mother Superior." Gridlock held himself erect and gazed up at the Pissoire ceiling whilst trying to look sanctimonious.

"How do I look now?" he enquired.

"Much better," beamed his tutor. "But don't forget to take small steps. Remember, you're a Bride of Christ."

"That's all very well for you to say Prunestone, you're used to it, you've had years of practice." They loitered suspiciously outside the public lavatory, while Phuckwytte changed into his usual odd assortment of women's clothing.

Having packed away their 'normal' clothes (if one could call them normal) they finally returned to the café to make enquiries as to whether any form of transport was available. Gridlock approached the nightshirt-clad patron and asked when the next available charabanc to Limoges would arrive.

"Thursday, Reverend Mother," the man politely pointed out.

"Christ Almighty! Bloody Hell! That's in four days' time!" barked Gridlock, whose outburst startled the clientele.

At this, Phuckwytte took his master to one side and whispered, "Look old chap, if you don't moderate your language and your voice, this entire 'Holy Sister' charade will be ruined."

"What the blazes am I supposed to do then?" the detective retaliated.

"Well, if you're in any doubt, just remember to keep your hands together, as if in prayer," recommended the doctor.

"I'll put my hands together round your bloody throat and then you'll be the one who's praying," Gridlock threatened as they departed with their luggage. So there you have it. A tall masculine unevenly breasted nun, sporting an eye patch, smoking a pipe and carrying a bag, a violin case and an Amazonian blowpipe, arguing loudly in English with a curiously dressed 'lady' complete with ginger handlebar moustache and matching wig, loaded down with heavy suitcase, ear trumpet and Gladstone bag. All this being closely followed by their local French emptier of cesspits.

"No-one will surely notice us," whispered Gridlock. "These disguises are foolproof."

It was 'Shit face' that finally came to the rescue regarding their transportation. But the experience of their previous calamitous journey by hay cart was to pale into insignificance by comparison to the mode of transport which the Frenchman now offered them, as it consisted of his ancient horse pulling his even more ancient cesspit wagon. This was made up of a massive steel tank that pivoted upon a wooden chassis, which could be, at the appropriate time and place, operated to release its vile contents, usually over arable land, quite commonplace in this area of France and England for that matter, ultimately producing lovely vegetables with a distinctive flavour. The approach to the owner's flyblown shed and stable became more apparent as the smell became stronger. Its location, not surprisingly, stood alone on the outskirts of the village. They politely refused their host's jovial offer of some homemade wine and waited patiently while Chemise, his mare, was backed into the shafts of their transport.

"I'm not climbing up on that thing, it smells awful!" Phuckwytte protested.

"It's that or walk," suggested Gridlock. "Unless you wish to play hide and seek with our circus friends until Thursday." They reluctantly joined their driver aboard the reeking, sewage-laden cart, and set off at a slow trot proceeding south, thankful for what little breeze came towards them as morning turned to midday.

"That's funny," remarked Phuckwytte. "The sun is out with not a cloud in the sky, yet wherever we go; we're always in the shade."

"It's the flies, Monsieur," said 'Shit face'. "In this heat they're a blessing!" The detective on the other hand was deep in his own thoughts about this complex case that he must solve at all costs.

These were interrupted by a distant rumble behind them, which became progressively louder as a horse-drawn circus caravan, travelling at speed, eventually came into view.

"Blast! They're on to us," cried Phuckwytte. "Can't this damn thing go any faster?" he shouted as several pistol shots were fired over their heads as a warning for them to stop. Their pursuers were now only yards behind them.

"Don't worry, Monsieur Spumes, pull that lever!" ordered 'Shit face', confidently giving a toothless grin. Gridlock did as he was told and pulled the lever hard, which immediately tipped the entire contents of the fetid tank into the path of their followers, which resulted in a temporary blinding of the horse, driver and passengers, causing the caravan to skid off the road, through a hedge and down a steep slope into a wood. Chemise, despite this spectacle, plodded on regardless.

"Well done, my friend!" said Gridlock, accidentally slapping the Frenchman on the back, and then looking for something to wipe his hand on.

"Good show, old man," chimed Phuckwytte. At this, 'Shit face' produced several bottles of his home brew to celebrate their victory, offering them to be sampled, but his kindness was politely refused. Undeterred, their driver continued to drink each bottle and throw the empties over hedgerows as they continued on their journey. Much later, it was a heavily inebriated Pierre that finally delivered them safely to the small sleepy town of Herpes-les-Pules that evening. According to 'Shit face', the town was renowned throughout France for the manufacture of string vests; these were actually made from old oddments of discarded string, (an early form of recycling). The inhabitants' regional costumes were entirely made of this material, down to their stockings, socks, shoes, hats and wigs. It was a stark reminder that eccentricity was not only an attribute of the English. When the Frenchman halted his cart, the two passengers descended with their luggage and thanked him warmly for all his help and generosity. They then bid him a fond adieu and watched him depart into the distance singing to himself and Chemise, followed by the buzzing cloud of insects.

Struggling with their possessions, the thirsty couple entered a local Auberge and ordered refreshment. The locals were surprised to see a ginger-moustached woman sipping Ricard, accompanied by a nun, quaffing down a litre of beer in one gulp. It seemed that the only lodgings they could obtain would certainly be offered at the Convent of Cystitis, situated on the brow of the hill on the other side of the village, to which the sorry looking pair wearily made their way before dark fell. Their destination was an austere grey stone building with a high walled garden and bell tower. They made their way across the courtyard to the enormous iron-studded front door, lifted a large iron ring and knocked loudly. Eventually the door was prised open by a young novice, who stared at them through thick-lensed spectacles as they introduced themselves. Her unfortunate protruding teeth caused her to lisp severely and the two were showered with spittle as she bid them welcome.

"Gentlemen, come thithe way, the thithters are now thinging at eventhong," she explained. "Pleethe thit down, the Mother Thuperior will thee you thoon…" She signalled them to sit and left to inform her superior, leaving the two men contemplating their surroundings, while wiping their saturated faces with their sleeves.

Finally, a large formidable-looking Sister arrived. Gridlock opened his mouth to introduce himself, only to be interrupted by Phuckwytte who blurted out, "My name is Lady Dorothy Fortescue-Blemish and this is my companion, Sister Uterus," he announced to the startled gathering. "We are at present engaged on an important quest of mercy," he whispered.

"Well, it's more of a pilgrimage actually," added a surprised Gridlock, attempting to imitate the piety of a saintly sister's voice. "We wondered if we could possibly beg accommodation for the night."

"We can pay our way," chimed in the doctor.

"That will not be necessary. We at the Order of Cystitis do not believe in financial rewards," replied their host, adding, "We pride ourselves on hospitality and sanctuary. Of course you may stay, but for that privilege, you will assist with various tasks by way of repayment."

"Sister Benedict Fumes here, will show you to your accommodation, and I will no doubt see you both at early morning mass," and with that curt order, she strode out into the corridor, her white starched flapping cornette sounding like a goose in full flight. They were given candles and shown upstairs to a whitewashed cell-like room. This was blessed with a small stained glass window, a bowl and pitcher and a small crucifix that hung above the simple single bed in which the two had to sleep.

As they listened to the bolt sliding and the key turning in the lock Gridlock snorted, "No need to ruddy well lock us in."

"Put it this way old chap, we're a lot safer in here than we were outside, for who knows where our pursuers are at present. I expect they're still looking for us at this very moment," observed Phuckwytte gloomily.

"What the hell do you mean by introducing me as Sister bloody Uterus!" exclaimed Gridlock with some degree of irritation.

"It was the first thing that came into my head," said Phuckwytte, expecting the usual cuff on the ear, and then justified his decision by admitting, "I thought it would help to enhance your femininity."

"That moronic head of yours is always filled with some kind of medical bloody clap-trap!" exclaimed his master. "So in future, kindly let me do the talking. Understand?"

"Yes, Sister," squeaked the doctor, "but might I suggest that you forego playing your violin. It might not be appreciated in this sanctuary of silence."

Gridlock ignored this witticism and suggested that as the bed was a single one, they would have to top and tail it. "I don't want to be kept awake by your incessant snoring," he advised. Despite this warning, however, Gridlock didn't get a wink of sleep, as his companion continually broke his vow of silence by his constant grunting, incessant snorting, talking in his sleep, smelly feet and continual visits to the chamber pot.

As predicted, there was a loud knock on the door at the pre-arranged time. Sister Fumes sprayed them a, "Writhe and thine," and led them to the Chapel where the others were reciting their rosarys.

"Christ, it's five in the bloody morning!" moaned Gridlock, who received a resounding, "Shush!" from those assembled. After mass they were given a frugal meal of raw radishes and mashed chickpeas, being finally handed mops, scrubbing brushes and sud-filled buckets and ordered to help clean the tiled corridors and toilets.

"I'm really not cut out for this menial work," complained Gridlock who was now on his knees, complaining that they hurt.

"Just keep on scrubbing," coaxed Phuckwytte.

"Blast! I've got indigestion from those sodding radishes," exclaimed Gridlock, and he belched loudly, which echoed down the corridor, much to the dismay of the others. After the allotted chores were completed, they collected their belongings, thanked their hosts and departed. Their short stay had felt more like a merciful release from a sentence of penal servitude.

Back in the town a large crowd of excited spectators, mostly women, were gathered waiting with eager anticipation outside the Hotel de Ville, which was now bedecked with tricolour string flags above which stretched a banner reading: 'The Great Montluçon to Limoges Bicycle Rally' under which was written: 'Health for All!' Herpes-les-Pules had obviously been chosen as one of the checkpoints for some sort of race that was due at any moment. Indeed one official was consulting his timepiece, whilst another shouted through a loudhailer, announcing the arrival of the first competitors. As our duo inched their way to the front of what was by now a very mixed and aroused female gathering, there came the distant sound of applause, cheering and screams, for around the corner sped a gaggle of naked male cyclists riding on tandems. The riders were wearing colour-coded ribbons tied in bows around personal and rather sensitive areas of their anatomy. It was assumed that these were worn specifically for the benefit of the more bashful female supporters, rather than as a means of team identification. Goggles were also worn, not only for the purpose of visibility, but also as an attempt to hide identification; while sturdy hobnailed boots were essential for grip. The affair was bizarrely French, being disorganised and noisy, but combining an elitist quest for health and fitness.

On arrival the competitors carefully alighted from their machines in as dignified a fashion as was possible, and then rushed straight into the hotel foyer in order to have their time cards stamped, sample the plates of fresh figs and to relieve themselves.

"We must seize the moment and knobble one of those tandems while the owners are inside the hotel," said Gridlock. "The problem is that our disguises look rather too obvious."

"Not if we take them off and try to blend in with the other competitors."

"I'm not taking my bloody clothes off for anyone!" shouted Gridlock, this outburst shocking the nearest onlookers.

"Look, old chap, we're not going to get very far carrying all this baggage, are we?" Phuckwytte pointed out. Gridlock begrudgingly relented, since they appeared to have no choice. Their only option was to make a dash for the hotel as quickly as possible, so that Gridlock could discard his disguise, while Phuckwytte packed away his best frock. This done, our two naked companions hurriedly availed themselves of plentiful pieces of discarded knotted string with which they tied their only possessions to the nearest vacated tandem.

"What about some coloured ribbon?" enquired Phuckwytte.

"If you honestly think that I'm going to decorate my manhood with coloured bloody ribbon, you've got another think coming!"

"Please yourself," replied the doctor as a blushing lady spectator complimented him on his matrimonial assets. They quickly launched themselves onto the cobbled street much to the amusement and appreciation of the crowd. Although some form of successful rhythm was achieved, it was not long before Phuckwytte began to complain.

"I I... t...think... w...we've m...mmade aa... bitt... of... a...aa... f...faux pax!"

"How...w ss...so?"

"T...These rr...ruddy c...cobbles aare p...playing h...havoc w...with m...mmy t...testacles," he moaned.

"J...ust k...kkeep p...peddling," ordered Gridlock as they continued on their way.

That afternoon all along the route, women shouted encouragement and waved their string undergarments – some of the more supposedly 'offended' affected to faint and were carried away. It was some time before Gridlock realised that in his panic to undress he had forgotten to remove his nun's headgear. Phuckwytte, still hurt by his master's constant criticism and cack-handed approach to things, had purposefully failed to mention this oversight and decided to use it as his only means of getting revenge. As the afternoon wore on they were inevitably overtaken by the rest of the pack, and were the last to reach the finishing line in Limoges by some twenty minutes. The prize-giving ceremony was well underway as a small assortment of amateur musicians wearing a hotchpotch of regional costumes, tortured the assembled gathering by playing a variety of instruments badly. Most of them appeared to be tone deaf and their tuneless attempt to play the national anthem was unrecognisable.

French roads, along with fatigue had left our pair with teeth chattering, eyes crossed and crutches numbed, and having now gathered momentum, they discovered that their brakes were virtually useless and that stopping was not an option. Passing the confused judges and racing officials, they continued through the town at high speed in the direction of the railway station, praying that a miracle would happen to relieve their situation.

"How far is this blasted station anyway?" enquired the doctor.

"Sod the station," replied Gridlock. "Let's just concentrate on trying to stop this infernal machine!"

Our intrepid pair had caused quite a commotion as they struggled out of control, on their increasingly distorted tandem.

"Watch out! Left, for Christ's sake! Steer left!" screamed Phuckwytte, whose attention was interrupted by the sudden appearance of a flock of sheep being herded across the road to the marketplace. A collision was inevitable. The pair were thrown off the speeding tandem as it made contact with the surprised animals and their shepherd. It was a soft landing for the cyclists, but not such a fortunate encounter for the woolly creatures. They retrieved the battered bike and raced towards the station to unload their belongings, where they would hopefully find somewhere to change back into their normal clothes. Modesty was inconceivable as they continued to cause chaos running naked through the crowded station onto the platform, looking for the gentlemen's toilet, much to the surprise of waiting passengers of the Paris train. In their wake, the furious French farmer was left shouting the most colourful French expletives, whilst gesturing wildly, as he attempted to gather up his frightened and precious livestock.

A collision was inevitable. The pair were thrown off
the speeding tandem as it made contact with
the surprised animals and their shepherd.

Chapter 7

Back to 'Old Blighty'

Now changed back into their everyday clothes, two tickets were purchased and our heroes boarded the Paris-bound train where they found an empty carriage. Gridlock at once sank into a desperately needed sleep, but after half an hour of counting the buttons on the leather seat out of boredom, Phuckwytte tapped Gridlock on the shoulder. The detective, who was unconscious by this time, woke and threw the doctor an irritated look with his patch-less eye, and muttered, "Christ! What now?" under his breath.

"Just to inform you, old chap, that I have to relieve myself and that I propose to search out a water closet for that very purpose," announced Phuckwytte.

"Thank you so much for that vital piece of information," came the terse reply. "Now, just get out and leave me in peace, you moron." Turning his head petulantly, the doctor left the compartment to relieve himself.

He swayed and lurched along two carriage corridors, continually knocking and bumping himself, whilst stopping regularly to re-adjust his hat and bustle. Half way down the second carriage to his utter amazement, he saw two fully-uniformed London

Bobbies standing side by side outside a compartment. The doctor bid the surprised policemen, "Good day," and peered into the smoke-filled carriage. He could hardly believe what he saw. Inspector Todger sat smoking the remains of a cigar, while pretending to read the *Le Figaro* newspaper that unknowingly he was holding upside down. Opposite him, handcuffed together, sat the Spiggotts and the German, Shortarshe Von Strumphe. He continued further on, found the darkened toilet, where he made use of the somewhat crude facility, and then tried to apply some more lipstick and rouge as the motion of the train rocked to and fro. Adjusting his clothes, he made his way back to the compartment where his companion had returned to a deep sound slumber. He shook the detective until he was fully awake, but on this occasion his irate colleague grabbed him by the throat with both hands and uttered, "Damn you, Prunestone!"

"Let me go, Spumes," cried the by now purple-faced doctor. "I have vital information."

Gridlock finally focused on the countenance of his companion. "Good God man! Have you been in a fight, what the hell have you done to your face?" he enquired. Phuckwytte looked at his reflection in the window. His application of lipstick and rouge, made him look as though he'd been in a calamitous road accident.

"Bugger this blasted train!" he cursed. Gridlock lost control.

"I suppose you're now going to give me a riveting full and detailed description of your visit to a French railway latrine! Pray tell me more. I'm fascinated."

"No, no," spluttered the doctor attempting to wipe some of the lipstick off. "Todger and two policemen have the Spiggotts and Von Strumphe under arrest. I saw them with my own eyes."

"Well, I didn't expect you to see them with anyone else's," Gridlock replied and calmed down, relaxing his grip.

"Come, we must go to them at once. Lead the way," he ordered.

Again, the doctor negotiated his way ahead through the swaying carriages, until they reached the two policemen, who immediately recognised the detective, and opened the door of the compartment so our pair could enter.

"Well, well, well, if it isn't Gridlock Spumes and his charming female companion," chortled the inspector. "Had you fooled, didn't I, my little rosebud, eh? What did you think of my 'Marcel' and 'Grizelda'? Not bad, eh? Though I say it myself."

"You failed to fool me, Todger," interjected Gridlock. "I realised who you were as soon as I saw the word 'Mum' tattooed on your forehead. Forgot to cover that, didn't you?"

Phuckwytte was shocked. "You knew all along that it was Todger, and you kept it secret from me and allowed me to suffer such appalling indignities? You really are unspeakable Spumes." At this, Gridlock and the inspector burst into laughter, congratulated each other on their skills of deception, whilst a crestfallen Phuckwytte took out a hankie and sobbed quietly.

"Anyway, it's good to see that you escaped from that vile crew. As you can see I managed to apprehend these pathetic specimens."

"Pafetik specimens, pafetik specimens! We ain't pafetik are we Reggie?"

"Na corst we're not sweet'art. We're just two innocents that's got caught up in this 'orrible affair. You've got no bleedin' right to arrest us," Eth complained.

"That's right, my little jellied eel," supported her husband. "We 'ad nuffin' to do wiv it. It wos this kraut wot done all Castrato's dirty work," and he gave Von Strumphe a sharp dig in his ribs.

"Nein, nein, zay lie. It vos dem in cahoots vid Castrato, not Herr Strumphe, I am a vigmaker to ze crowned heads of Europe! Got ein himmel!" He then launched into a tirade of German. But Gridlock silenced the unidexter by asking Todger how he had managed to escape and arrest the three criminals he now had handcuffed in his care.

"Well," said Todger, "I was being held down and kicked by half a dozen of those circus ruffians, when my two trusty police officers, Sergeant Worms and Constable Gropeworthy here, made a gallant rescue attempt and saved me." The two policemen nodded at his approval.

"After that it didn't take long to track down these three idiots."

"We ain't idiots," cried Eth.

"Shut up," threatened the inspector and continued, "Anyway, a message on the Continental Wire Service from Yard Intelligence has informed me that the ringleaders are possibly holed up somewhere in Tooting, therefore we must work out a plan of action forthwith before we reach England."

"Agreed," said Gridlock.

"Don't worry," Todger expressed confidently. "We'll have the blighters behind bars eventually."

The rest of the journey through the night was spent in much discussion and argument, as they worked out a complicated scheme to apprehend the villains on their return. However, by the time their train pulled into Victoria Station the following morning, after a calm Channel crossing, none of them were any the wiser about what to do next. The three handcuffed prisoners were bundled into an omnibus by Todger and his officers, and they headed straight for Scotland Yard, while our companions hailed a hansom cab, which ambled its way through the rain-swept streets to Baker Street.

Once there, they gave the door three good loud knocks and waited in the pouring rain for the door to be answered. After some minutes they could hear the slow but steady sound of wood hitting floor tile, as down the hall corridor a limping Lilly approached, cursing and swearing in her usual manner. Bolts were unbolted, latches were unlatched, and chains were unchained. The door opened gradually and the wrinkle-stocking clad, unsmiling, Lilly appeared.

"Ah, Lilly!" exclaimed Gridlock, "How lovely to see you again. It's so good to be back home. Isn't that right Prunestone?"

"Spot on Spumes, old man. No place like home."

"Never mind all that, flattery ain't goin' to get you nowhere," she muttered, spitting out what remained of a crumpled hand-rolled cigarette. She then wiped her nose with the back of her hand and scratched her backside. "Suppose you'd better come in," she said begrudgingly, and beckoned the two drenched men inside.

"Thanks for tellin' me you was comin'," she complained. "Expect you wants feedin'. Bloody inconvenient if you ask me. Take off them wet things and wipe yer feet before yer goes upstairs." And with that, she trundled her way back into the kitchen. Phuckwytte noticed that she was walking even more slowly than usual and then observed that her under drawers had come adrift and were down round her ankles, or at least her remaining one.

"I say Gridlock, do you think we ought to mention the fact that her fallen drawers could cause her a mischief?"

"Listen… Do you want to be the one to tell her?"

"Not really," admitted the doctor, visualizing what commotion that would cause.

"Well for God's sake shut up then!" his master snapped. "Her fallen drawers have always caused her mischief. Let nature take its course. Survival of the fittest and all that." The two colleagues shivered their way upstairs to the sitting room and collapsed into two leather armchairs, by the miserable excuse of a smoky fire.

"No place like home, eh?" muttered Phuckwytte, blowing into his cupped hands for warmth. "And this certainly is no place like home."

Lilly entered minutes later, bearing a breakfast tray that contained a plate piled high with burnt muffins, and a pot of lukewarm liquid that was her idea of tea.

"I've brought you this morning's paper," she announced.

"Thank you Lilly, you may go," said her employer.

"I wos goin' anyway," she replied and left the room with suppressed laughter.

"Good God!" exploded Gridlock, sitting bolt upright his one eye bulging at the leader headline in *The Times*, which he read out loud:

"'National Pubic Hair Collection Stolen'." Phuckwytte's face adopted the same amazed expression as he listened to his master, who continued with the startling news.

"Listen to this: 'In the early hours of yesterday morning a daring robbery took place at the Victoria and Albert Museum, where a highly professional criminal gang managed to break in and remove from several display cases the nation's priceless collection of pubic hair'."

"Cricky!" exclaimed the doctor as his master continued:

"'The much prized collection, (some of which is reputed to be over 1500 years old) contains the follicles, not only of the Kings, Queens, and Aristocrats of England, but also Archbishops, Politicians and their various wives and mistresses'."

"Great heavens!" cried Phuckwytte as Gridlock read further:

"'It is rumoured that the collection was originally started by King 'Odo the Bald' in 700 A.D'." Scanning the page he read on:

"Blah, blah, blah… Ah, listen to this bit. 'However, more recent specimens stolen include samples from Queen Victoria; Prince Albert; Mr Brown and Disraeli. Sir Carey Hunt the well-known spoonerism and curator of the museum was quoted as saying: 'These offending scoundrels need to be brought to justice! This robbery surpasses the Great Wart and Dandruff Theft of 1856 and is a national tragedy, since these priceless pieces just cannot be replaced'." Gridlock put the paper down, thought for a moment and then it dawned on him.

"Castrato!" he blurted out. "This robbery has her signature upon it. Everything falls into place. Occasionally it doesn't, but in this case it definitely has. What a fool I've been."

"Yes, you have," admitted Phuckwytte.

"Of course!" continued Gridlock. "Castrato! That bloody woman needed to get me out of the country and into some God-forsaken corner of France, together with Scotland Yard's top man, Inspector Todger, so that she could instruct her spies to carry out this ghastly crime, whilst she inveigled us by sending us on a wild goose chase. God only knows what fate they had in mind for us. Death or incarceration, I have no doubt," Gridlock raged.

"And with us out of the way they could carry on with their evil plans unchallenged. Well my dear lady, you have failed to shake off the great Gridlock Spumes. For I will do for you, just as I did for your twin brother, who even now is languishing in the Tower of London at Her Majesty's pleasure." At this point the angry detective paused and drew deeply on his pipe only to discover that it was empty and that he was out of tobacco yet again.

"Of course, it's quite obvious what will happen next, and I will wager a pound packet of Bassets Best upon it. For while Todger and the Metropolitan Police are busy searching Tooting and the rest of London for the perpetrators of the pubic hair robbery, Castrato will no doubt launch a daring raid to release her infamous brother from the Tower. Find her my dear Prunestone and you'll find the stolen collection," he concluded.

"We must go to Scotland Yard immediately. Todger must be warned of this."

"I'll slip into something more suitable," said Phuckwytte, and a few moments later he swept into the room in a revealing sparkling sequined silver ball gown with matching shoes.

"Bloody hell, Prunestone, you look like a damned fairy queen! We're just going to Scotland Yard, not The Hunt Ball at the bloody Ritz."

"I don't care, you never know what high-ranking police officials may be there, and in any case, we're meeting Inspector Todger and I thought you, or at least he, might be pleased to see me looking my best."

When the two men arrived at Scotland Yard they found the inspector at his desk in a small dismal room, surrounded by wooden filing cabinets, and with a large map of London pinned on the wall covered in little flags. He was eating a great doorstep sandwich filled with tripe and onions, most of which was deposited on his chin. He took a slurp of some stewed tea from a chipped enamel mug and belched loudly.

"Ah, Spumes and Prunestone," he said while masticating furiously. "Sit down gentlemen," and the inspector flashed a seductive wink at the doctor, who blushed with embarrassment.

"I assume you have acquainted yourselves with today's headlines 'The Great Pubic Hair Theft', and presume that is why you're here. Well don't worry, I'm one step ahead of you, and have already despatched a sizeable detachment of policemen to deal with the problem and to track the villains down. It's only a matter of time before we have that devil, Gonad Varicosi and his mob, clapped in irons. Fancy scrawling his name all over the walls of the museum before he escaped. The audacity of the man – pure ruddy vandalism."

"This has nothing at all to do with Gonad bloody Varicosi," announced Gridlock, now incensed.

"This is the work of Castrato and her henchmen. It is my belief that this whole thing was a ruse to keep the police busy whilst she attempts to rescue her brother Biryani from his imprisonment in the Tower." The inspector took a huge bite from his sandwich that caused its contents to squirt down the front of his shirt.

"Sod it!" he cursed, wiping it into the material with his handkerchief. Chewing methodically, he eyed the detective up and down, wiped his mouth, sat back in his chair and lit an old cigar butt.

"You know, Spumes old man, I hate to admit it, but you could just possibly be right. I've worked on over twenty cases with you now, and you've come up trumps on every one. How do you do it? That's what I'd like to know."

"I just put together my genius in forensic science, combine it with my unparalleled skills of detection, and, of course, my mastery in the art of disguise, and there you have your answer Inspector," replied Gridlock.

"Not forgetting a liberal coating of modesty," muttered Phuckwytte under his breath.

"Come, gentlemen, we've not a moment to waste. Check your revolvers. Todger, I suggest that you recall your men at once and have them sent straight to the Tower. This time, by George, we shall lay in wait and nab them," cried Gridlock, rather over-dramatically, in Phuckwytte's opinion.

The guardians of the Tower had immediately been informed by telegraph of their impending arrival, and preparations had been made to disguise Gridlock and Phuckwytte as Yeomen Warders (commonly known as Beefeaters) in the traditional costume of dark blue with red trimmings, borrowed from those not on duty. Todger had also summoned Worms and Gropeworthy to assist him, since they were already involved in the case; while Scotland Yard's finest were dispatched and placed strategically about the fortress that was once a Royal Palace. Once the pair had changed into their colourful and historic uniforms, the five of them rushed to the White Tower where they had been informed that Biryani was incarcerated. The group tiptoed to the appropriate chamber and Gridlock pulled the door observation hatch slowly back and peered into the lockup.

"Thank heavens, he's still there," he whispered as he squinted through the gloom at the figure sitting upright at a desk, with his back to the door, and who appeared to be reading.

"Now, all we have to do is to set our trap and surprise his would-be rescuers. Come gentlemen, we will place ourselves in the empty room next door and wait." Indeed, this did prove to be a long one, (5,134 yards, 8 feet, 3 inches to be precise) but during the three days it lasted, they persevered and occasionally whistled, stood on one leg, and sometimes laid down in order to pass the time. This was followed by a hopping contest; guessing how much change each other had in their pockets; and counting the moles on each other's legs.

After this interesting lengthy interlude, extreme boredom took over, which lead to much carping and complaining by his disillusioned companions. Under pressure, Gridlock decided to go ahead and face Biryani alone, while the others waited. Perhaps he could gain some helpful information with a little careful interrogation, face to face. He rose slowly, adjusted his sheep's-wool moustache, (for disguise was paramount), changed over his eye patch from right to left, donned his Beefeater's hat and proceeded to Biryani's cell. Once outside he peered through the inspection hatch again. Yes, sure enough, there sat the professor, no doubt planning his next villainous crime. Quietly he opened the door with the huge key he'd been given, and once inside slammed the door shut to surprise the occupant. The figure in front of him remained seated, without a trace of acknowledgement.

Standing behind his old adversary, he exclaimed scornfully, "So, we meet again professor. Only this time in a place you so thoroughly deserve to be. You were warned not to cross swords with Gridlock Spumes and now you are paying for the consequences. No doubt you're waiting to be rescued by your notorious sister and her criminal gang of cutthroats!" Gridlock was now enjoying the moment as he moved forward slowly.

"Oh yes, my dear Biryani, we are aware of her plans." He clasped the prisoner by the shoulders with both hands and shook him, whereupon the head became detached, fell forward onto the table, and rolled across the floor.

Shocked at this spectacle, Gridlock's keen mind now realised that it was a carefully constructed life-like waxwork dummy. Its body now toppled from the chair and fell awkwardly, landing in an unnatural position. Dumbstruck, Gridlock picked up the head, complete with string beard and leather wig, and hurled it across the room in anger. The life-size mannequin was clothed in a black morning coat, waistcoat, trousers and shoes. Inspecting the exposed opening of the torso, he then began to rip out the padding that consisted of several copies of explicitly illustrated risqué under-the-counter magazines.

"The perverted monster," muttered the detective as he selected a couple of the finest examples, stuffing them down the front of his tunic. Rummaging in the torso's coat pocket, he found a bill of sale from Harrods Knightsbridge for Foie Gras and Truffles; a gentlemen's pocket-size book on *How to avoid knee-trembling whilst courting in the wild* by Dr Hamish Gadaffi; and instructions on *Icelandic bee keeping*: 'start with one bee'; along with a crumpled message recently scrawled in smudged red ink. 'Sorry I couldn't be here to give you this note in person. Once again I have outwitted you Spumes. You really are proving to be a rather numb-brained and unworthy opponent. There is something that may be of interest in the waistcoat pocket, apart from the magazines, for which I know you hold a fascination. Regards Biryani.'

Gridlock contorted his face into a grimace, which could only be described as resembling a bulldog licking urine off a nettle. His opponent appeared to know far more personal things about him than he cared to admit. Pocketing the evidence he proceeded to look through the dummy's waistcoat, finding a metallic object, which on inspection appeared to be an exquisitely engraved silver snuffbox, set with precious stones. Flicking the small catch, the lid of the box flew open and therein, set snugly inside on a velvet cushion, was a cluster of black curly hairs. A small printed label on the inside of the lid read: 'Sample from the body of Henrietta Haddock, mistress to Lord Copious Mucus 1710.'

"The filthy swine," cried the overwrought detective, and shouted for the others to join him. They entered and Phuckwytte, shocked at what he thought was a headless body, began to cry histrionically. The inspector took him to one side and tried to console him.

"Now, now, my brave little soldier," Todger comforted. "Don't upset yourself so. We can't have one of Her Majesty's Yeomen Warders crying like that, can we now?" And with that, he gave the doctor his tripe and onion soaked handkerchief, along with a knowing squeeze of the hand, and turned to the detective.

"You were quite right in your assumption Spumes. But we're too late – he's made us look like brainless halfwits."

"He's a good judge of character. These unspeakable villains have crossed my path once too often. My blood is up, my knees are down, and heads will roll!"

And with that, our raving leader, (taking care not to reveal his purloined literature), plunged his hand into his long john's, removed a handful of liquorice allsorts from the secret inside pocket (which due to the contents having melted had caused an unsightly stain), and stuffed them into his mouth. Kneeling to attention, he then swallowed hard and saluted, while attempting to sing 'Rule Britannia'. He then stood up plunging his index finger into his right nostril, and proceeded to hop up and down the cell at an alarming rate.

"Heavens!" exclaimed Inspector Todger. "Does he often do this?"

"Sadly, yes," was Phuckwytte's reply. "He told me in strict confidence once, that he's never been the same since he returned home from active service in India. Hostile tribesmen, loyal to the 'Great Khazi', captured him in the Ammu Shitloo Mountains in Kashmir. He was gathering intelligence, and by jingo, the British Army needed some at that time. Despite this, they tortured him, stripped him naked, painted his testicles with a mixture of yogurt and fresh chilli, tied one foot behind his back and put a placard around his neck which read: 'Queen Victoria very bad King. Long live The Great Khazi.' The blighters then made him hop backwards to his barracks in the blistering midday heat.

"Good Lord," roared Todger. "That man has really suffered up the Khyber."

"Indeed," concurred the doctor, as he stared pityingly at his friend's demented gyrations. "Your Khyber would suffer under those terrible conditions."

Slowly Gridlock emerged from his stupor, delirious. He raised himself to his full height and muttered in a strained voice, "Gone, gone and never called me mother," and then began to sing the hymn 'For those in peril on the sea' in strained falsetto tones. Phuckwytte sat him down and offered him words of comfort, but his deranged master threw them straight back to him. Eventually the doctor managed to calm the overwrought detective, fearing for his mental state of mind.

"There, there old man, calm yourself down. We'll soon have the blighters under lock and key," he soothed.

"I'll have my men take the dummy back to the Yard, but in the meantime don't worry," Todger said reassuringly, but he was stopped in his tracks by a commotion, which erupted from the courtyard below.

"What the blazes!" he cried as they both wondered what all the shouting and clamour was about.

"Good Lord, what's going on down there?" Phuckwytte exclaimed.

Before anyone could answer, Sergeant Worms burst through the door breathing heavily, with a look of grave consternation on his face.

"Sir, sir," he cried. "It's a disaster."

"What man, out with it, speak up!"

"The Tower of London's priceless collection of Tudor codpieces 'as been nicked, purloined, thieved and 'alf-inched."

"Good grief!" growled the inspector. "First pubic hairs, and now codpieces. Where's it all going to end? They could be miles away by now."

"No, sir," replied Worms. "Impossible, 'cos as soon as the codpieces was lifted, so to speak, the security alarm bell was rung and all exits were immediately shut down."

"How come that we didn't hear it then?" asked Todger.

"It's a silent bell sir. We needed to keep an element of surprise and didn't want to warn the villains that we're on to them sir."

"Good man, Worms," congratulated Gridlock, feeling better at last. "I can deduce that since you've been so rapid in your response in shutting down all the exit points, there is now an extremely high likelihood that our quarry still remain on the premises."

"Hoorah, bravo Spumes," said the doctor jumping up and down with excitement. "Brilliant, clearly your superb powers of deduction have not deserted you!"

"Elementary, my dear Prunestone," he replied. "We will now search every nook and cranny of this historic pile until we entrap these blighters. Come gentlemen, there will be no escape for them this time."

As the others eagerly dashed down to the courtyard below in search of their prey, the detective decided to search The Central Armoury famous for its display of weapons, shields, and a unique collection of body armour through the ages. Once inside, he instinctively felt for his revolver.

"Damn! I've left it in my coat pocket," he muttered as he advanced slowly and silently amongst the great suits of armour. He was now sweating so profusely that this, combined with his nose running, affected what remained of his spare cardboard moustache that now drooped, looking much the worse for wear, since he'd discarded his woollen one that had itched terribly and made him sneeze. A sudden peal of laughter rent the air, causing him to stop suddenly. Perusing through the display of evil-looking weaponry, he decided to arm himself with a rather magnificent 15th Century two-handed broadsword. He lifted the weighty weapon from the brackets that held it to the stone wall, and with both hands attempted to raise the mighty blade above his head. Sadly, he had not considered just how heavy it was and when the weapon had been fully hoisted, the sheer weight of it toppled him backwards, causing him to fall on his back. The distant peal of laughter began again and turned into uncontrolled giggling. Gridlock raised himself up, took up the sword and proceeded to where he thought the laughter was coming from. Stopping abruptly, he heard someone singing in an Italian falsetto voice. It was coming from the giant suit of armour in front of him. Taking out his magnifying glass he scrutinised the exterior with a professional scrute, and noticed what looked like sauce that had been accidentally spilled on the burnished steel breastplate. He ran his finger through the substance, smelt and then tasted it. It was a delicious mixture of garlic, tomato and Parmesan, while an appetising smell came from within.

Strange, thought Gridlock as he rested his eyes upon the helmet, for they were very tired. Studying the display information plaque below, it read: 'This armour was made at great expense for Sir Crispin Clenchbuttock who died of acute cowardice at the Battle of Grande Fosse Septic at Grosse Excrement. 1335.' It was then the detective noticed a piece of toilet paper protruding from the helmet's visor, which he withdrew and read the brief scrawled message, again written in red ink: 'In case you're taken short. Have gone to ground. Better luck next time!' signed 'Castrato'.

"Curses!" Gridlock's face reddened with anger as he stuffed the note under his tunic. But what was that delicious aroma? He stood on tiptoe to investigate. Gently lifting the helmet's visor, he peered inside to discover a man cooking pasta.

"Pleeze, pleeze, donta kill me," came a terrified voice, and sure enough, hiding inside the huge suit of armour was the height-challenged, golden-toothed Italian kipper vendor.

"Pleeze signor, dey'a force'd me to 'elp them. I'm'a suppose'a to be on'a look out, but I was'a 'ungry," he pleaded.

"I've got bigger kippers to fry than you, you little Italian creep," cried the detective and with that, he slammed down the visor and hearing voices again, continued to tip-toe forward, dragging his heavy broadsword behind him.

He cut a strange figure as he crept forward amongst the displays of steel weapons. The sound of a woman's laughter now echoed from the end of the room. Gridlock was now beside himself with rage at being duped yet again. The laughter stopped suddenly, whereupon a series of muffled flatulent sounds followed. A vaporous mist began to rise at the far end of the gallery and he recognised the vile odour, which grew stronger as he moved forward, causing him to hold his breath. Through the mist he could just make out the shapes of three figures, dressed as Beefeaters, inching their way to the exit, carrying a small trunk.

Methane, Castrato and Biryani! The blighters are disguised like the rest of us. So that's how the devils got in! he thought to himself and then let out a blood-curdling cry.

"Gridlock and St George! Into the breach once more dear friends!" By now he was striding feverishly ahead like a man possessed, his heavy sword smashing into the displays of steel armour as he turned at each corner. The noise was deafening and his progress was slow, but Gridlock's determination was undiminished as he advanced towards his quarry. In the distance his enemies were making good their escape, despite being hampered by the heavy trunk that they dragged behind them. Gridlock at last dropped his cumbersome weapon and dashed forward, out into the blinding sunlight and fresh air.

By now so many bona fide Beefeaters were scurrying about, it became impossible to decipher who the real culprits were. In the ensuing confusion he ran down the steps to the lower ramparts and out through the Middle Tower Gate at the west exit, towards the river. It was then that he tripped and fell flat on his face, grazing his hands and knees in the process. Exhausted and depressed he sat down on an embankment bench, put his head in his hands and wept. *That bloody woman, her wretched husband and her devious twin brother had foiled him, once again, and had literally vanished into thin air.* These thoughts were all too much for him and he began to twitch uncontrollably as the others arrived from different directions.

Embarrassed by their presence, Gridlock attempted to pull himself together and croaked, "Gentlemen, any luck?" They shook their heads.

"They must have escaped through 'The Traitor's Gate' and got away down river," deduced Sergeant Worms.

"On the contrary, that gate has been locked for years," Todger corrected.

Depressed at being foiled again, they returned to the guard's room to hand back their costumes and consider their next move.

"Why anyone would wish to steal and own such a bizarre collection of our English Heritage beggars belief. No doubt these precious relics were stolen to order and my guess is that they will eventually find their way out of the country – you mark my words," exclaimed the inspector gloomily.

"But what I don't understand is how those villains managed to disappear so quickly," sighed Gridlock, while reading the handwritten note again. Then finally it dawned on him and excitedly he leapt out of his seat.

"I've got it! I've got it!" he shouted.

"Well for Christ's sake don't give it to me!" remarked Phuckwytte dryly.

"Enough of your cheap sarcastic puns, Prunestone."

"They're not cheap, they're costing me a fortune!" the doctor complained.

"Well it hasn't been much of an investment has it?" came the answer.

"I knew it," the sleuth cried, waving a piece of toilet paper in the air. "'Have gone to ground' she's given the game away, without realising. Gentlemen, follow me!" and he rushed outside, down to the river, as the others struggled to keep up with him.

Gridlock returned to where he had fallen, breathlessly exclaiming, "Just as I thought."

"But I don't understand sir," said Constable Gropeworthy, carelessly swinging his truncheon and smacking himself in the face as he did so.

"The trouble with you policemen is that you don't think on your feet, bearing in mind that they're big enough," Gridlock scoffed. "Please observe," he continued, pointing to the ground. "In my extreme haste to apprehend the suspects, I tripped over this manhole cover, stubbing my toe in the process."

"Very careless of you," replied Phuckwytte without sympathy, instigating a strong look of disapproval from his master who continued, "This cast iron manhole cover has not been replaced in its original position, as you can see. Luckily for us, in their careless panic to get away, the blighters left it in this dangerous state, whilst making good their escape down into the sewers." He lifted the cover to reveal a ladder which disappeared into the darkness below.

Phuckwytte began to panic. "You're not suggesting for one moment that you expect me to go down there, are you? There are rats down there as well as all kinds of unspeakable filth. I've already suffered the indignity of travelling for bloody miles on a French flyblown cesspit wagon and now you expect me to go underground and wade through the English equivalent!" he now shouted hysterically. "This ruddy case is the most shit-ridden I've ever been involved in!"

Dear reader, he has a point, so far one has to agree with him.

Chapter 8

Bravely into the bowels

They commandeered kerosene lanterns and waders from the Tower storeroom.

"I'd better inform my superiors at the Yard of our position and seek agreement to continue our investigations," cautioned Todger.

"We have no time to waste by tangling ourselves up with bureaucratic nonsense," interjected Gridlock. "These blighters already have a twenty-minute lead on us, for God's sake."

Phuckwytte reluctantly tucked his ball gown into his pantaloons and moments later they were descending down into Joseph Bazalgette's labyrinth of amazingly engineered tunnels designed to remove London's waste. This subterranean world was a frightening experience for those of a nervous disposition, making Phuckwytte a prime candidate. To him, it was not unlike descending into the 'Jaws of Hell'. As the group continued down, the atmosphere became clammy, with a mixed smell of dampness and untreated sewage. Floating above the fetid, slow moving contents, a layer of mist prevailed in every direction.

"Blimey, it doesn't half pong down here," Phuckwytte complained.

"It's supposed to, it's a sewer," replied Gridlock. "In any case the contents are produced from a good old-fashioned English diet! There's none of your 'Johnny Foreigner' muck down here," he announced proudly.

"Oh look! There's a fork in the tunnel. People will throw any accoutrements down the lav," joked Gropeworthy, whose attempt at humour was met with indifference. The beam of Gridlock's light caught the shape of something floating towards them.

"What the hell is that?" cried the terror-struck doctor. "It's not a dead dog is it?"

"It's all right, it's only a Beefeater's hat," the detective noted. "We're on the right track, and they can't be far ahead of us now."

With renewed enthusiasm they increased their pace. For over an hour they continued until the tunnel widened into a chamber, and they were now faced with tunnels leading off in three different directions.

"Now what do we do?" asked Phuckwytte.

"We had better separate," suggested Todger. "You and the doctor take the central one. Worms, you take the left and Gropeworthy and I will take the right." He shone his lantern and scrutinised the constable. "Do that top button up! Where the hell do you think you are?"

"In the shit, Sir!" answered Gropeworthy adjusting his tunic.

"Precisely," came the reply.

"But we'll get lost and never get out alive," cried Phuckwytte starting to panic. Just then a huge rat swam past him and he cried out hysterically, "This is no place for the likes of me." He now resembled a pregnant ballet dancer in waders.

"I can't stand this claustrophobic shit hole any longer," he screamed.

"Shut up you ninny and listen," Gridlock ordered.

"I'm fed up with listening – this continual running water makes me want to go."

"Well you're in the right place," smirked Worms.

"Be quiet and listen, for God's sake," said Gridlock. A faint tinkling sound could now be heard in the distance that slowly increased in volume, as a medieval leather codpiece with little bells attached to it floated towards them out of the right-hand tunnel.

"It looks like part of a jester's outfit," observed Phuckwytte.

"You should know, Prunestone," came the curt reply.

"It's part of the stolen collection, all right. They must have dropped the trunk and sprung the lid open," said Todger fishing it out and giving it to Worms as evidence.

"Onward to the right, then gentlemen," announced Gridlock. "We'd better try and speed up."

"It's all right for you lot," Phuckwytte complained. "You don't have a sequined ball gown stuffed down your underwear."

They struck out once more and appeared to be climbing gradually in a northerly direction, although it was difficult to tell and at one point they swore that they could hear voices. But then, the mind can play tricks in an underground sewer. Sometime later, however, they did hear someone singing 'Come into the Garden Maud', a popular tune of the day. For round the next bend they came across a sewer-hunter. The little man was sieving through the muck, wearing a stained canvas sou'wester, a long greasy coat and trousers over his boots.

"What you lot doin' down 'ere?" the 'Tosher' demanded. "On yer 'olidays?" he joked. "It's no good tryin' to identify yer own, it all looks the same down 'ere mate."

"We haven't come down here to identify 'our own', as you so charmingly put it," remarked the detective.

At that, the man spat a tobacco-stained gob against the wall and eyed Phuckwytte lecherously. "You're an 'ansom woman aint'cha?" and carried on sieving.

"We're the Metropolitan Police," Todger explained officially.

"Blimey!" came the reply. "They're recrutin' theatricals now."

"And who might you be?" enquired Gridlock.

"Ned Flusher, mate. I does the sewers round 'ere," and he held out a stained-gloved hand to be shaken, which was understandably ignored.

"Cours't I wasn't always a sewer 'Flusher' down 'ere yer know. Originally I trained to be a brain surgeon, but I couldn't get to grips wiv' the Latin, mate."

"What's that big stick for?" enquired Phuckwytte.

"Clubbin' 'the bunnies'."

"What!"

"The rats."

"Oh."

"You must find all sorts of things down here," remarked Gropeworthy.

"You wouldn't believe what treasures I've come across't down 'ere over the years. Candle ends, buttons, the odd glass eye. I've even got a collection of dentures at 'ome," he said with pride.

"Yer know, I found a leg down 'ere once, an' it weren't a wooden one either!" The group were shocked at his gruesome admission.

"I see that you come prepared and wear gloves," observed Worms.

"Well, it stops yer bitin' yer nails," Ned replied, giving his sieve another shake. "Ah ha! What's this!" he cried raking through the excrement. Finding a coin, he wiped it on his sleeve and held it near the light.

"Excuse me for asking, and I don't mean to stop you working, but how do you know where you actually are down here?" enquired Todger.

"By the paper matey, by the paper. I'm a connosewer, mate. Get it!" he chuckled spitting again. "Yer see, yer refined individual sheets means they are high class toffs, probably up Belgravia an' Mayfair way, whereas yer pages of old newsprint or anythin' yer can get hold of's, more workin' class, and you're under Bermondsey or Wappin' in the East End."

"How fascinating," remarked Gridlock sarcastically. "What an intellectually stimulating and charming life you must lead."

"Yern mate," Ned replied.

Gridlock came straight to the point. "Have you seen or heard anyone else down here?" The man thought for a bit and chewed off a bit of tobacco from a wad in his pocket.

"Fancy some baccy?" Gridlock wisely refused. "Well I don't know, but I could' a sworn that I 'eard some splashin' and a lot' a swearin' an' coughin' about ten minutes ago up towards Marylebone way."

"That'll be them!" Gridlock was as excited as a gun-dog picking up the scent of a rabbit, which under the circumstances would have been impossible to detect above the pungent aroma which prevailed.

"Oh well, better get off 'ome," said Ned. "I've got to get down river an' put the cat out."

"Why's that?" Phuckwytte asked.

"It's on fire, mate," laughed Ned as he bid them farewell and continued on.

Our team of criminal experts began to gain momentum encouraged by the good news.

"Looks like we're gaining on them at last. We'd better check our arms and ammunition and keep silent. This could be messy."

"It couldn't be much messier," observed Phuckwytte, as the few sequins left on his gown were now tarnished, most having fallen off, leaving a glittering trail behind him. Eventually they came to an immense chamber of intersecting tunnels, from where the sounds of the world above could be heard.

"We must be under either Baker Street or Marylebone Road. Here, look at this," Todger exclaimed finding a fragment of dark blue cloth caught on the rusty ladder which lead to the surface. One by one they climbed up into the daylight, only to find themselves in the middle of a dangerously busy thoroughfare. They were in fact now standing opposite 'The Baker Street Bazaar' that exhibited the famous Madame Tussaud's waxwork collection.

"Of course! It all makes sense," cried Gridlock exclaiming, "The dummy of Biryani in the Tower, that's the link!"

"Great Scott!" cried Phuckwytte.

"Are you of course referring to me?" questioned the detective.

"No. I just said it to enhance the story," the doctor replied with a smirk. "That, and knowing what a modest, shy and retiring fellow you are," he continued with meaningful sarcasm, as he was understandably depressed, weary and dishevelled.

"Don't try and be funny, Prunestone. I get what little laughs there are in what's left of this chapter," Gridlock scoffed, giving his usual look of disapproval. "And not at my expence either!" he shouted, while nearly being run down by the brewer's dray.

As our sewer-soiled group attempted to cross to the opposite pavement, they were aware and embarrassed that pedestrians were giving them a wide birth. Some discretely held handkerchiefs to their faces and darted hurriedly away, while even a stray dog started to draw attention to them by barking, only to suddenly squeal loudly and rapidly make off down an alleyway.

Red-faced but undeterred, our brave comrades finally managed to enter the exhibition building.

Chapter 9

Who's the dummy?

An old woman at the kiosk gave Gridlock a gap-toothed smile as he approached and asked, "Family ticket love? That'll be a tanner ducky, only you'll 'ave to 'urry, we're closin' in 'alf an hour."

"We're not a family, actually."

"Thrup-ens fer you an' yer lovely missus then," she said eyeing Phuckwytte's distressed gown, which caused him to blush.

"I'm not married to this gentleman!" said Gridlock sharply.

"'Ave you trodden in somethin'?" she sniffed.

"We've just had a day out down in the sewers," informed Phuckwytte making things worse.

"Now listen here Madame, we are the Law," Todger announced.

"Gawd 'elp us," she exclaimed. "I ain't done nothin' wrong, honest."

"No, no, Madame, of course you haven't," agreed Gridlock. "It's just that we're looking for three men carrying a trunk."

"Well actually one's a woman," admitted Phuckwytte.

"So," she said, "carryin' a trunk's not an offence is it? Where did yer get that gown from dearie? It's in a bit of a state, ain't it? Suits yer though – matches the 'andbag." She looked down. "Pity about the waders though." Gridlock was now becoming impatient.

"Who might you be?"

"I does the tickets, love."

"And what's your name exactly?" he asked.

"Dolly Belcher, Mrs Dolly Belcher to you," she replied brusquely.

"Where's the manager?" the detective enquired.

"Any one of three pubs round 'ere 'avin' his oysters an' Guinness. Why?"

"Look, this isn't getting us anywhere. We've no time to look for him," he snorted, and marched past her into the exhibition hall, as the others trailed behind.

They were now in a richly decorated and mirrored lobby where the lone seated waxwork figure of Madame Marie Tussaud sat so life-like – it could have been the old lady herself. Behind this was a separate room aptly named 'The Chamber of Horrors', displaying all sorts of gruesome characters. They were all there. Len Porridge, 'the Sidcup Strangler'; 'Halitosis' Jack 'the mad axe man from Stoke Poges'; Gilbert Hole, 'the Eastbourne rapist'; Boris Fruit, 'the Norfolk goat molester'; and Doreen

Squirt from Budleigh Salterton, who caused thirteen innocent people to commit suicide by giving a seventeen hour lecture on the mating habitats of owls.

"I don't like the way the eyes follow you around the room," said Phuckwytte nervously.

"Don't worry old man – you'd look like that if you'd been stuffed!" Gridlock commented. His frown now deepened as he paced up and down. The doctor, knowing better than to interrupt his master during such moments of thought, gestured to the others to keep silent. Gridlock finally ordered Phuckwytte and Todger to search the first floor, while Gropeworthy and Worms should go to interview the staff. And with that, they all rushed off to carry out their respective tasks, leaving him alone to wander about the tableaux of past royal families.

Meanwhile, on the first floor Phuckwytte and Todger searched the historic displays. They were drawn to an extremely realistic scene of 'The death of Lord Admiral Horatio Nelson'. The spectacle consisted of a busty Lady Hamilton, splendidly dressed as Britannia 'ruling her waves', as she hovered above the dying Nelson, who was being kissed by Captain Hardy.

Looking up at Lady Hamilton, Todger confessed, "She's a buxom wench if ever I saw one. She looks so real." And the two of them climbed onto the plinth for a closer inspection. Phuckwytte contemplated the benefits of having such a bosom, and as he studied the life-like texture of the skin, he distinctly heard Nelson cough, which caused Captain Hardy to sneeze in his admiral's face. Todger and the doctor glanced at each other suspiciously, and it was at that moment that Phuckwytte received a sharp poke in the rear from Britannia's trident, and as he screamed in pain, Todger was hit smartly over the head with her shield and laid out cold. The three historic waxwork figures then fled from the podium.

Hearing the screams and commotion, Gridlock dashed up the stairs and into the upper gallery where he found the unconscious Todger and a panic-stricken Phuckwytte, who was jabbering incoherently to himself.

"What the hell has happened?" he demanded. Phuckwytte, while inspecting his damaged backside was in no state to give an immediate answer.

"Out with it man!" barked the detective.

"I… well… It's, it's, they…" Phuckwytte stammered, "they just came to life!" he cried.

"Who?" Gridlock demanded.

"Nelson, Captain Hardy and Britannia."

"Don't be so bloody stupid!" Gridlock shouted.

"It's true, it's true, I swear," pleaded the doctor. "Britannia clouted Todger over the head with her shield, look at the dent in it!"

"But what in God's name made you cry out like that?"

"You would scream with the prong of a trident shoved up your arse!" protested Phuckwytte. At this point Todger regained consciousness, blew his whistle to alert his men and passed out again.

"Which way did the blighters go?" asked Gridlock.

"Through those curtains," Phuckwytte pointed to the backdrop.

When the others arrived they managed to revive their superior and proceeded with haste through the back of the display that led into workshops and to the costume wardrobe, which was stacked full of wigs, false noses, glass eyes and all the necessary items needed to produce the figures on display. While searching, Gridlock discovered a fine white silk handkerchief that had been dropped on the floor in haste, by the side entrance. On the bottom right hand corner was a hand-stitched gold initial 'B'. He discreetly slipped it into his pocket while the others searched through all the strange paraphernalia that was heaped in drawers and cupboards. Finding no evidence, they finally ventured out of a side door which led them to the bustling street outside.

Meanwhile, ahead of them, the three hunted criminals, having taken flight were now safely ensconced in the snug bar of 'The Maggot & Parrot', a nearby public house situated round the corner, where they had pre-arranged to meet a certain high ranking official. Moments later a tall, thin, melancholy, white-haired man dressed in black and wearing a stove pipe hat appeared in the doorway. He could well have been mistaken for a mortician, which had in fact been his previous profession. However, his career had now led him to a much grander and more lucrative way of life, as he was now more involved with the pleasures of the living than those of the dead.

"You're late!" he announced angrily.

"Actually we were here before you," replied the professor, which was ignored.

Seeing the strangely-clad accomplices the man was clearly not impressed. "Why are you dressed like that? This isn't a bloody carnival!"

"Excuse me, but who exactly are you?" enquired Methane, annoyed at the man's condescending attitude.

"I'm incognito," replied the contact.

"Well, there's no need for your pompous attitude Mr Cognito, we're all on the same side and you're amongst friends here. I'm sorry if there's been some delay, but Inspector Todger and the police are in hot pursuit," he explained. At this, the man produced a pistol and held it to Methane's head.

"You blundering idiot! Not 'Knackers of the Yard!' If he has word of what we are up to and where we are, I can assure you, that you and your associates will die."

"Don't panic," said Bulimia as she attempted to pacify their contact, carefully moving the pistol away from her husband's temple as she did so. "We have the merchandise stored in a safe place at the rear workshop of Madame Tussauds. Kill him, or us and you won't get a damn thing."

"My master does not like to be kept waiting," said 'the man in black'.

"When do we get paid?" asked Biryani. "After all, we're the ones who have taken all the risks."

"You'll not be reimbursed until we receive the promised goods."

"In that case, we cannot do business unless we deliver the goods personally," was Biryani's reply.

After some thought the man reconsidered. "I will have to seek agreement from my superior. However, he will be most displeased when informed that Scotland Yard has been alerted." At this point 'the man in black' gave Methane a slip of folded paper.

"You will need this in order to decipher a coded message in an article which will be placed in tomorrow's copy of *The Illustrated London News*. The article will give you the place, time and date of our next meeting." He then left the room promptly, without uttering so much as a goodbye. Methane gave a sigh of relief and read the message on the paper to the others.

"'One ounce of black shag, one cottage loaf, two pounds of Brussels sprouts, six ounces of potted shrimps, two radishes and a hair net.' This is a bloody shopping list!" he cried. Bulimia took the list turned it over and handed it back to her brother.

"Bloody stupid place to put it! It's on the back," he complained. The message read: 'Look in the gardening section for your instructions' and that was all.

The detective had decided to call it a day.

"It a day?" he called, but nobody replied. They had searched the Tower of London, waded through the city's sewers and ransacked Madame Tussaud's waxworks museum, without success. He was hot, tired and hungry and needed rest. Having returned home, Phuckwytte was dispatched to buy some liquorice allsorts, as the police went back to the Yard to do what they always did – lie in wait. Sometimes they stood in wait; sometimes they even sat; but they always reverted to lying down again.

Gridlock tried to relax in a hot bath, (a rare treat) that Lilly had prepared for him. He lit his pipe and scrutinised the purloined silk handkerchief under his magnifying glass, but that, along with his monocle, began steaming up and he couldn't see a thing. Disgruntled, he finally got out, put on his red Chinese silk dressing gown (with a gold embroidered dragon on the back) and went into his study to inspect the evidence; lighting the oil lamp on his desk, and turning up its wick to get a better look. The handkerchief was of the finest quality white silk and the gold letter 'B' had been exquisitely hand stitched with genuine gold thread. An item of quality, no doubt belonging to a person of rank. He placed the article in the desk drawer, as a soaking wet Phuckwytte entered.

"I see that it appears to have been raining," Gridlock observed. "I trust that you've got them?"

"Yes," announced the doctor, and threw a large bag of his master's favourite confectionery at him, the wet bag split open spilling its contents all over the floor.

"I'm now going to change my clothes, if you don't have any objection," he said curtly and with that, he left the room dripping a trail of water behind him. On his hands and knees, Gridlock salvaged what he could of his precious allsorts, popped half a dozen into his mouth, sat in his favourite armchair and began to cogitate, a painful experience at the best of times. To whom did the handkerchief belong and who had dropped it in such a hurry? The perfume was surely that of Bulimia and if so, it would indicate that they had missed their target by only minutes. He decided to keep this theory to himself for the time being until he was more certain of the facts.

The next morning Methane purchased *The Illustrated London News* from the little newspaper shop next to Mortimer's tobacconist in The Strand. In it, under the gardening section was an article entitled 'Nude Composting Can Be Fun!' in which he read to himself the following message: 'Nude composting during the summer months can be a **meeting** of like minds and **this** can afford enormous fun combined with productivity. The exercise will offer your neighbours a visual treat as you undertake to pile waste matter into a heap, working until **evening**, when sadly the midges tend to go for one's nether regions, which under the circumstances, of course, lets the **side** down. One should take great care whilst bending, as you compact your organic material in layers. A compost receptacle can easily be made from an old wooden **door** or crate. For the less adventurous composters amongst you, working at night should only be attempted whilst **wearing** carpet slippers, so as to not wake the neighbours. One should also be equipped with a hurricane lamp and a **black** umbrella, held by an accompanying gardener. This is advisable **only** if it rains.' Once deciphered, the instructions in the article were now clear. 'Meeting this evening, side door wearing black only'.

Later that evening there was a loud knock on the side door of the workshop. Once opened, it became obvious why instructions had been given for their dress code. Their mysterious contact now entered with his accomplices, carrying an empty coffin, which they placed on top of a workbench. Bulimia closed the door behind them as they then proceeded to unscrew the coffin lid in order to remove it. Their contact asked, "Before you place the precious things inside, I wish to make sure that they are genuine and intact."

Biryani and Methane produced the trunk that contained the stolen cod-pieces, while Bulimia fetched the pubic hair collection from the cast iron safe. After 'the man in black' had studied its contents with some care, the items were transferred to the casket and the lid was replaced, secured and carefully covered with a black cloth. Now sealed and covered, they silently carried it out and loaded it onto a hearse that was bedecked with all the solemn refinements of a stately funeral. The horses' bridles were brightly polished, and their black-feathered headdresses swayed in the breeze, and the carriage work and windows gleamed.

"Since you wish to remain with the said items until payment, you will be required to act as pallbearers. I have been instructed to place you in a separate carriage ahead of the procession, which I will drive personally. My colleagues will follow behind in the hearse." The three were then handcuffed and locked inside the leading carriage.

"A precautionary measure," 'the man in black' assured. They finally set off at a slow pace down Baker Street, through the descending fog – a solemn sight amongst the misty shadows of the city.

Todger, ever suspicious, had, for once displayed some foresight and instructed Worms and Gropeworthy to join him in keeping the museum under surveillance. As the bogus funeral procession passed by, Sergeant Worms was authorized to alert Gridlock at his rooms, while the others continued. But before this occurred, Constable Gropeworthy (who like all good Bobbies, happened to have a piece of chalk amongst other oddments in his trouser pocket) was instructed to draw arrows on the pavement indicating the direction in which the cortege was travelling, in order to aid Gridlock's pursuit of them, as they had to immediately leave, to keep up their observation.

Chapter 10

The mastermind is revealed

Sergeant Worms pulled the door bell of the detective's abode sharply and after several moments the door was unbolted. Phuckwytte appeared in the doorway dressed in lady's night attire, complete with hairnet and fur slippers. His face was covered in a lurid green beauty cream.

"I have to care for my complexion," he explained, realising that his appearance had startled the unsuspecting sergeant. He then slowly negotiated the stairs, asking the policeman to wait in the study as he reluctantly made his way to the detective's bedroom, aware that his master would not be best pleased at being woken from a well-deserved rest. After the usual verbal outburst at being disturbed, Gridlock sprang into action, ordering that they both dress, without delay.

"Hmmm, let me think," pondered Phuckwytte. "Shall I wear my crushed red velvet with puffed sleeves or, I know! What about my pale blue Little Lord Fauntleroy outfit, for a change?"

"I don't give a fig what you put on, just hurry!" snarled Gridlock. The pair dressed hurriedly, with the doctor in usual outlandish female attire. They checked their revolvers and rushed out to follow the trail of chalked arrows. It was at the junction of Oxford

Street where they finally caught up with Todger and Gropeworthy.

They continued on, making their way through Mayfair towards Piccadilly Circus. Throughout this area they encountered occasional groups of 'Ladies of the night' who offered their services at every opportunity. One in particular sidled up to Gridlock in the hope of some 'trade', remarking, "I can see you're a gent of great penetration sir. Fancy a quickie?" which he tried to ignore.

All around them, obligatory drunks staggered about from dive to dive, and toffs and their escorts made their way from theatres and music halls in the vicinity. At this point the fine drizzle that had been falling for the past half an hour now became a shower. Phuckwytte as usual began to complain about being wet, how the rain was spoiling his hair and that in haste, he had forgotten to change from his slippers which were now letting in water.

"For God's sake, will you just shut up for once in your life, you whingeing little pansy!" barked Gridlock.

"It's alright for you, but my feet are killing me and I'm soaked through," whined the doctor.

"I'll join your bloody feet in sympathy and finish the job for them, if you don't shut up!" retaliated the detective as the funeral procession headed down through the Haymarket and into Trafalgar Square.

"Where on earth could they be going at this time of night?" Phuckwytte asked.

"If we knew that we wouldn't be standing here in the pissing rain!" responded Gridlock.

"Well I only thought…"

"Look… Just do me a favour. Don't think!" the detective snapped back at him.

Turning down into Whitehall, in an attempt to relieve the strained atmosphere, Todger announced, "What we need is some decent transport and some extra help," and with that, he rushed off and disappeared.

Some moments later the funeral procession turned right into Downing Street and circled round at the front of three stationary landaus that were waiting in line outside Number 10. After ten minutes of intense observation from our stalwarts, various high-ranking politicians and cabinet ministers, including the Prime Minister, emerged from the building and boarded the waiting transport. The cortège then proceeded in the direction of the Houses of Parliament. At that moment, a Metropolitan Police Black Maria carriage appeared and hurriedly made its way down Whitehall towards them. Instead of horses within its shafts, the vehicle was pulled by four bare-footed panting police constables, with their boots tied together and hung around their necks, (silent running being a priority). They were being 'driven' so to speak by Todger, who commanded, "Whoa," for them to stop.

"Gentlemen be my guests, please get in at the rear," as Todger smiled down at them from the driver's seat.

"I say, what a wizard idea," said Phuckwytte, brightening up at last. "What happened to the horses?"

"No time to harness them from the stables," admitted the inspector. "Anyway, there's nothing like good old Scotland Yard for manpower!" he chortled and they all laughed.

"This way we can travel in silence too!" The two of them climbed aboard, but Worms and Gropeworthy were ordered to take off their boots and join the others. Todger cracked his whip and they were off again.

Up ahead in the front carriage, as the bell of Augustus Pugin's clock tower chimed midnight, it seemed to be a signal for the rain to cease.

"Sounds like Big Ben," said Methane, stating the obvious.

"Really, you don't say. I thought it was that gold Hunter of yours," remarked Biryani sarcastically.

"Oh for God's sake, stop it you two!" Bulimia was now angry at the continual bickering between the two of them which had been going on since they left the museum.

"I'm bored just sitting here."

"And I'm hungry," moaned her husband.

"You're always bloody hungry!" she snapped.

"I haven't eaten since that cold beef and pickles we had for lunch," he grumbled, and thereupon emitted yet another most unwelcome occurrence.

Biryani produced a handkerchief from his breast pocket, covered his nose and threatened the offender, "If I could only get out of these wretched handcuffs, I'd stuff a cork up that offending rear end of yours, drag you back and stick you in that ruddy coffin and bury it as deeply as possible, you unsavoury little turd."

"No need to get personal," exclaimed the crestfallen Methane.

"For the life of me Bulimia, I can't understand why you married such a flatulent anatomical freak," complained Biryani to his sister. Their raised voices now caused concern and their captor banged on the roof signalling them to be silent.

It was generally assumed that they were now somewhere south of the river and they were at present passing under a bridge. The sound of the horse's hooves on the cobbled street had now changed to an echo. Apart from that, they had no idea where they were.

Methane broke the silence and asked, "Any idea who this 'collector' fellow is? He seems to be a rum kind of cove."

The professor shrugged his shoulders. "I don't know. All I can say is that we'll have to play things their way for the present and no doubt we'll know soon enough. Obviously, they will need to verify the authenticity of the goods, as they represent part of an invaluable historic collection. Although, having said that, they're not likely to be forgeries, but one never knows. In any case, most of the famous contributors are now dead, so one only has the official label to go by."

"I couldn't tell the difference between a male and a female pubic hair, let alone who it belongs to," remarked Methane, who lost control yet again, much to the dismay of all concerned.

"It wouldn't be so bad if we could open the bloody window," Biryani complained.

"Normally he blames it on Rasputin our Irish Wolfhound," his sister replied caustically.

Some distance behind, our heroes followed, unaware of the bickering and sniping taking place ahead of them.

"I must say old chap, there's nothing like being transported by the Metropolitan Police. This is what it must be like being taken to Bow Street to stand trial," remarked Phuckwytte, now in a lighter mood as he was drying out.

"If only that were true in your case," remarked Gridlock, who by now had suffered quite enough from his companion's incessant jabbering about clothes, his coiffure, shopping and countless other trivia. All Gridlock wanted to do was to focus on the problems in hand. Who had died, that warranted such important people to attend their funeral? Why the devil were the Prime Minister and other dignitaries now part of a funeral cortege in which arch-criminals were involved? And who was the original owner of the handkerchief that Bulimia had dropped? His thoughts were abruptly dashed, as Phuckwytte demanded that they should now halt the carriage in order that he might relieve himself. He had been chatting continuously since they left Southwark to take his mind off the dilemma.

"Certainly not," retorted Gridlock angrily. "You'll just have to control yourself, be a man for once in your life and wait."

"B…b…but," spluttered the doctor.

"No buts."

"But for how long must I wait?" he pleaded.

"If I knew where we were going, I could tell you, but till then, I'm sorry. You'll just have to hold it."

"But Gridlock!"

"Look, tie a ruddy knot in it will you, if we lose sight of our prey, we will never reach their destination or discover who the mastermind is behind all of this," said Gridlock unyieldingly.

As usual, Phuckwytte began to sulk and after some moments, feeling uncomfortable, he began to tap his feet. As they approached Jamaica Road, he suddenly stood up and burst into a rendition of 'A rollicking band of pirates we' from Act II of Gilbert and Sullivan's *The Pirates of Penzance*, which then prompted the team of running, straining constables to join in, sending Gridlock into an uncontrollable rage.

"What in damnation do you think are you doing?" he shouted.

"It takes my mind off things," shrieked Phuckwytte as he sat down, crossing and uncrossing his legs in an attempt to stop the inevitable. Inspector Todger on the other hand was quite impressed at the choice of popular song from the D'Oyly Carte Touring Company which had just made its debut. He decided to add his deep baritone voice to the performance, which continued on for the rest of the journey throughout Bermondsey. Other pieces of opera attempted included Verdi's *La Traviata*, Mozart's *Cosi Fan Tutte* and a selection from Puccini's *Madame Butterfly* (strange as it was yet to be written in 1903). Gridlock was surprised at the doctor's vocal versatility, but by this time Phuckwytte's bladder finally gave way and despite the attempted distraction of his inadequate musical repertoire, he stood up and relieved himself through the bars of the window, sending out a steady steaming stream into the darkness which was met by curses and obscenities shouted by soaked pedestrians. After this unfortunate occurrence they eventually reached Rotherhithe and then turned left down into Church Street, heading towards the river. But instead of alighting at St Mary's Church, in order to bury the deceased in the graveyard, as one would have expected, the procession continued further on and finally came to a halt outside of an octagonal building with a canopied door in front. Next to this was what appeared to be a workshop or pump-house that supported a large chimney.

Meanwhile, the first carriage of the funeral finally stopped and their captor alighted, unlocked the door, released his captives, inviting them to step down. They were then ordered to help the others to unload the hearse and assist in carrying the coffin, which was followed by the group of notables from Downing Street. This done, 'the man in black' then directed the procession into the large Rotunda. Gridlock and his companions arrived just in time to witness the strange gathering disappear into what they recognised as the entrance to the once celebrated Thames Tunnel.

"Cor blimey, strike a light, I'm bleedin' knackered!" Constable Gropeworthy exhaustedly exclaimed, as they lowered the shafts of the Black Maria. Gridlock stepped out of the vehicle and joined the doctor.

"Funny place to have a bloody funeral isn't it?" he said. But before an explanation could be offered, a steady stream of hansom cabs, hackney carriages and phaetons, could be seen approaching in their direction.

"Quick men," shouted the inspector. "Hide this damned thing round the corner. Come gentlemen, let us follow and observe from where we cannot be seen." The group were now hiding with heightened excitement and anticipation beside the deserted 'Spread-eagle & Crown', a riverside public house. Carriages continued to arrive and depart after depositing their passengers at the embankment. During the following hour, well over twenty vehicles had come and gone. The distinguished passengers all in evening dress began to exchange pleasantries and slowly they proceeded into the entrance of the octagonal building.

One by one the visitors passed through a brass turnstile that was manned by an enormous hulk of a man who, as the visitors entered, touched his forelock while offering his hand out to receive a small gratuity, and on receipt of their calling card, in a grave voice, he announced their arrival. By the light of a nearby gas lamp, they could just see his rough features. The shape of his baldhead resembled that of a large baked potato under which was carelessly arranged a broken nose and cauliflower ears. To complete the picture, he had the swollen eyes, protruding cheekbones and the toothless smile of a bare-knuckle fist fighter. Closer and braver inspection would have revealed a heart with the word 'Doris' beneath it, tattooed on his Adam's apple. The gargantuan was squeezed into a tweed suit that was at least three sizes too small for him. Every time a lady or gentleman passed him their identification, his anvil-sized hand took it. He would then read out, with some difficulty, the names of the guests.

"The Right Honourable Bertram Moist and Lady Abundance Grope... Rear Admiral Horatio Snodpule... The Maharajah of

Hindu Krutch and party… His Excellency the French Ambassador, the Marquis Paralyses De Crotchcott…"

The name calling went on and on. The great and powerful were all present. Politicians, senators, men of law and medicine, celebrities from the world of theatre and dignitaries from the far flung corners of the Empire.

"My God," whispered Phuckwytte. "A pretty impressive gathering. The deceased must be somebody of great importance. What do you think? I mean, they can't just be going through to the other side of the river to bury the poor soul."

"Of course not, you dunderhead," growled Gridlock. "Something jolly important is about to take place… Perhaps it's some sort of celebration, but why here? This is very bizarre. Something is definitely amiss, Phuckwytte, and I don't just mean you."

This usual put down fell on the doctor's deaf ears, as Gridlock suggested that once the gathering had entered, that they should gain admittance somehow, but how to get past the vast hulk guarding the entrance?

"I've got it!" said Todger.

"God, not you as well!" mumbled the doctor.

"My men will rush the bruiser and overpower him."

"I don't think so," replied Gridlock. "A small army would be required to move that heavy weight brute from our path… Ah! I have it!"

"You've already had it!" cried Phuckwytte backing away.

"Prunestone old chap. You must commit suicide in order to distract him. Naturally when he notices your dilemma he will be more than willing to assist you, and when he does, we will enter unhindered. A damsel in distress, how could he resist it! What do you think my friend?"

"What do I bloody well think?" replied the doctor in shock. "There's no soddin' chance, that's what I bloody well think! How dare you even suggest such a rash and dangerous thing? Just because I have a penchant for wearing ladies' clothing, it doesn't mean that I will use my obvious charms to indulge in such a charade. My answer is no! Absolutely not!"

"We'll take that as a yes then," replied Gridlock. And with that, the others all pleaded and begged the doctor to proceed with the plan, since it appeared to be the only obvious solution to the predicament in which they found themselves.

Phuckwytte finally acquiesced under pressure (along with placing money in his hand), hoisted his skirts and crept to the river's edge only yards away, taking care not to be noticed by the pugilist. He then adopted what he considered to be a suitably melodramatic pose and began to sob loudly, with the back of one hand on his forehead. This produced no reaction whatsoever, so he began to improvise his performance by waving his arms about and introducing further over-emotional dialogue.

"I cannot go on, I cannot go on!" he ranted at the top of his voice.

"Oh, wretched life! Woe is me! It's the time to end it all!" He was by now beginning to enjoy the sensational experience and he became even more hysterical.

"Oh, cruel world, I will say goodbye forever, the muddy waters of 'Old Father Thames' beckon to me. I will end it now and throw myself into the river!"

"The bloody idiot, what the hell does he think he's doing?" asked the inspector.

"Damned drama queen, I'll throw him into the bloody river myself," grumbled Gridlock.

"Hush," whispered Todger who was quite impressed. "Look, our friend has left his post and is approaching our little Ophelia."

The thug slowly walked down to where Phuckwytte continued to rant and rave. As he moved towards what he thought was an attempted suicide, he spoke softly so as not to cause fright.

"Now, now dearie yer don't want to be jumpin' into that filthy ol' cesspit of a river. You'll catch yer death of cold an' gawd knows what else. Nuthin'k can be that bad, surely. Wots a fine-lookin' woman like yerself got to be un'appy about? Come on now dearie, give us yer 'and and come wiv old Charlie-boy. We'll 'ave a glass or two of gin an' you can tell me yer troubles." With that he attempted to grab the doctor's arm, but Phuckwytte stepped sideways and the bruiser stumbled forward losing his balance and as he did so, Phuckwytte struck the gent a sharp blow on the head with his parasol, and a sharp kick on his rump completed the business. The Samaritan fell face forward into the black grimy Thames.

"'Elp, 'elp!" Charlie screamed, in between going under and swallowing copious amounts of the noxious water. "I can't bleedin' swim, for gawd's sake 'elp!" he shouted and down he went again weighed down by his heavy boots and clothing. Upon surfacing he coughed and spat out more water. "I woz tryin' to 'elp you, you bleedin' old tart, now you ruddy well 'elp me!" he shouted.

"Hmmmph... I might have done if you hadn't called me a bleedin' old tart," replied the petulant Phuckwytte, and he waddled away from the drowning man.

As the doctor joined Gridlock and the others at the entrance, they all congratulated him on his acting display.

"Capital, splendid, sterling stuff old boy," remarked Gridlock.

"What a performance – I doubt if even our great Ellen Terry could have done better," said Todger. Flushed with pride, Phuckwytte savoured the moment, but was struck by a sudden twinge of remorse.

"Oh my God! What have I done? That poor man... come, we must save him." They rushed to where the man had fallen and ran up and down searching for some sign of life. As they looked, a gurgling sound, followed by the word "Muvver," was faintly heard by the would-be rescue party, whose eyes were drawn down river where they caught sight of an arm and then a hand disappearing into the murky waters. All that remained was the bruiser's bowler hat that danced too and fro on the water that was finally caught in the outward current. Phuckwytte took out a lace handkerchief and began to wail and sob in earnest.

"Come now, we haven't got time for all that, what's done is done, no use crying over spilt beer," said the inspector.

"It's milk, actually," replied Gridlock. "You cry over what you like mate, but I could do with a nice jug of ale right now. I've got a thirst like a dead bear's bum."

"What's that like?"

"Bloody 'orrible! Come on, let's continue our investigation and get down into that tunnel."

Once through the unmanned turnstile the party moved into what had once been a luxuriously appointed entrance. The interior had now deteriorated and the once colourful frescoes and decorations were in a sad state of decay. They hurried down the steep flights of steps that cantilevered out from the perimeter wall, and entered through one of the arches that formed the actual entrance to the tunnel itself. Each of the sixty arches from end to end had originally been lit with gaslights, most of which were now not in use, but those remaining seemed only to add to the general dank and gloomy atmosphere. Designed by French engineer Marc Brunel and his English-born son Isambard, what had once been considered to be 'The Eighth Wonder of the World', complete with entertainment and commercial enterprise, was now deserted; the shops were closed up, and although the pedestrian walkways remained, the tunnel was now mainly used for carrying freight and the odd passenger by steam train. There were no signs of life and an eerie silence prevailed.

"They've got to be somewhere here – our villains can't just disappear," thought Gridlock aloud.

"I don't like it," retorted Todger.

"We can't change it now, it's the only one we've got," confessed Gridlock.

"Truncheons out lads!"

"Beggin' your pardon Inspector, we ain't got no truncheons, we left 'em in the van," informed Sergeant Worms.

"Well, just try to look menacing, and don't forget the self-defence and advanced crochet techniques that you've been taught." Gridlock removed his revolver from his coat pocket. Todger removed a half-eaten corned beef sandwich from his and the doctor took out an ivory handled nail file from his clutch bag and held it menacingly.

"Right, men!" ordered the inspector. "Proceed in single file, and not a peep out of anyone." They inched their way along the tunnel until distant voices were heard. Todger halted abruptly, and the men who had been following in close order, were taken by surprise, causing the inevitable collision. They clambered to their feet and proceeded silently until the voices became a little more audible. Just ahead were two large doors (the nearest being partially open). The room inside appeared to be brightly lit. Gridlock whispered to the group to split into two and stand at either side of the nearest door with their backs to the wall.

The voices could now be heard quite clearly and Gridlock recognised them, all but one that is. It was a deep, cultivated voice that seemed to direct the conversation.

"Now, would you kindly open the coffin and allow me to observe the contents."

"First, there is the small matter of payment – ten thousand pounds to be precise. We would like it in used notes now if you please, or we take the stuff back."

"Professor Biryani!" whispered Gridlock.

"All in good time," 'the man in black' replied.

"That time is now," replied Bulimia's voice. The familiar sound of anal retort resulting in an odious stench made its way through the doorway.

"Bloody Methane!" coughed Todger. And with that, the party took evasive action, covering their noses – apart from Gropeworthy who for some unknown reason covered his eyes. As our heroes struggled for breath outside, the lid of the coffin was being carefully removed to reveal its contents.

"Oh, superb, utterly superb!" said a voice.

"You have done well. My master will be delighted with this magnificent collection. He is expected here within the hour and I am sure he would be pleased to thank and reimburse you in person. Now if you would be so good as to follow me…" The sound of voices and footsteps disappeared and was followed by the slamming of another exit door.

The investigators took no time at all to enter a large room that had once served as some kind of store or pump room. It had now been magically transformed into what one could only describe as a gaudy, yet luxuriously appointed, bordello. Its brilliantly lit chandeliers were suspended from a mirrored ceiling – the new power of electricity being run by some kind of generator. They were struck dumb. Their mouths opened wide and eyes bulged as they took in the scene before them. Persian and Indian carpets covered a marble floor. Luxuriously upholstered sofas and the odd chaise longue lined the edges of the room. But the sumptuous décor was not what was holding the men's interest, for almost every square inch of wall space was covered with drawings, paintings, prints and photographs which could only be described as pornography of the most explicit kind. Interspersed between these erotic representations were displayed strange artefacts from around the world. Most appeared to be connected to strange fertility rights, but others were obviously designed to illicit some kind of exotic pleasure. Many were not so easy to comprehend. Statues, large and small depicted every kind of sexual activity. Whips, chains, masks and strange devices were laid upon tables along with items of weird apparel. The men slowly began to move around the exhibits and to scrutinise them with great care.

"Gawd's strewth!" "Soddin' 'ell," and "Bleedin' 'eck," came the response, along with, "Blimey, I didn't know that woz possible."

"Look at the size of this Sarge!" and, "The missus will never believe me!"

"Silence, you frustrated perverts!" shouted Todger, vexing his displeasure at his men. "Sergeant Worms."

"Yes guv."

"Will you control these idiots, I don't want anything touched. This entire collection of filth and degradation will be confiscated and removed."

"Where to, guv?" the sergeant asked.

"To my office at Scotland Yard – where the hell do you think!"

"Right, guv," came the response.

The inspector continued, "I intend to study and catalogue them meticulously at my leisure." This caused Sergeant Worms and Constable Gropeworthy to grin and wink knowingly at each other. Their superior noticed this and at once ordered the two men to replace a set of highly indecent French postcards, which they had purloined, or face immediate dismissal. Worms and Gropeworthy grudgingly removed the offending articles from their uniforms and put them back on the display.

"We must track down the filthy swine who has amassed this disgusting collection of ghastliness," gasped Gridlock. "It is precisely this kind of muck and outrageous behaviour which is slowly but surely polluting the wholesome spirit of this great country of ours!" He then made a closer inspection. "I must say though, that these Rowlandson prints are exquisitely drawn Phuckwytte."

The doctor was oblivious to the comment as he was now fumbling through a collection of ladies' lingerie and undergarments.

"It seems that you are taking a little too much interest in those particular items," the detective sneered.

"I'm only looking," replied the doctor. "I find them most fascinating from a purely historical point of view. God knows how women got into some of these things."

"Or out of them," replied Gridlock as he fingered a 13th Century leather chastity belt. Prunestone's eyes fell upon a glass display case and he began to study its contents. All manner of strange and outlandish paraphernalia was arranged within. Some of the objects defied his imagination, and after some moments of contemplation, he gave up and walked to the other end of the room where he came across the opened coffin.

"Hurrah!" he exclaimed clapping his hands excitedly. "I have found what we have been searching for! Over here, Gridlock. Look, look!" He became so enthusiastic that he began to perform a little ballet he had choreographed from *The Nutcracker Suite*.

"Quite enough of that," said the detective. "Save your theatricals for when we're at home." He removed his tartan eye patch, took out his cracked and grimy magnifying glass and peered into the casket. Todger and his men crowded round in anticipation. Gridlock, placing his eye patch back again announced, "Well gentlemen, this is the evidence we've waited for, and with luck we shall have the bounders behind bars before you can say 'Jack Robinson'."

"Who's he?" asked the doctor.

"How the hell do I know!" came the response. Just then, the group froze as the distant sounds of laughter, giggling and chattering voices were heard approaching from the tunnel.

"Quickly, everyone hide where you can and observe, but don't move or make a sound until I give the order," whispered Gridlock. The men scrambled to find hiding places. Gridlock closed the door quietly and squeezed himself behind a sofa, which was standing in front of a screen of heavy curtains, behind which Prunestone and Todger had already positioned themselves. The door was then flung open and the sound of merriment increased as ladies and gentlemen of all shapes, sizes, and of all ages crowded into the room. All were attired in their undergarments.

The men in long johns remained booted and wore nothing else except their moustaches, beards or the occasional monocle or pince-nez. Most were smoking and drinking. Their female companions had dispensed with their usual underskirts and lace-up whalebone corsets, in order to encourage freedom of passage. They wore scanty cleavage-enhancing bodices above their lacy knee-length bloomers. Black silk stockings and elbow-length gloves seemed to be the order of the day. An abundance of precious jewellery completed the effect.

The observers in hiding were almost knocked unconscious by the heady mixture of perfume and tobacco smoke, as they watched champagne corks popping, as several white-wigged velvet costumed flunkies proceeded to offer glasses of bubbly to the partially inebriated revellers. Kissing, fondling and embracing among the group was now underway by all concerned. Some made their way to the sofas; others were content to take advantage of the floor coverings. A good deal of outrageous behaviour began to develop which slowly turned into a full-blown no-holds barred orgy. As the sofas groaned under the weight of the pounding revellers, our spectators were in fear of being suffocated or discovered. Half a dozen musicians then entered carrying their instruments and began to play the well-known and much requested 'Burlington Bertie'. 'The man in black', whose voice Gridlock hadn't previously recognised, strode to the middle of the room and announced, "My Lords, Ladies and Gentlemen, please be upstanding, if you are not already in that agreeable state! Ha, ha, for our beloved patron, known to us, his confidantes as 'Dirty Bertie', your 'Royal Master of Ceremonies, Edward the Caresser'!"

He took a huge gulp of bubbly, puffed at his Havana cigar and proclaimed, "My dear, dear guests, I see some of you have begun without me," as much laughter ensued.

The band then struck up a fanfare as two flunkies opened the other door and in strode the man himself. The short rotund Bertie marched into the room followed by what appeared to be a gaggle of giggling and scantily dressed girls, which prompted much applause from an appreciative crowd. The Royal Subject was adorned thus: around his Royal shoulders, a black velvet cloak bore his Royal Coat of Arms. His Royal chest was resplendent in a low-cut vest, out of which Royal chest hairs protruded, while a large corset supported his enormous Royal stomach, which was offset by a ruffled tutu. Under this, a black leather codpiece contained his Royal 'Crown Jewels'. Pink tights of the purest silk covered his Royal legs and his Royal feet were squeezed into a pair of gold dancing pumps. Before he commenced he stepped forward, threw his black top hat to one of the girls and to another his opera cloak.

He took a huge gulp of bubbly, puffed at his Havana cigar and proclaimed, "My dear, dear guests, I see some of you have begun without me!" as much laughter ensued.

"I shall have to make up for lost time, but before I do, I have something of a surprise for you all." Clapping his podgy little hands together, two of his staff entered the room carrying a strangely shaped object covered by a gold and crimson cloth. They set it down by the Prince and stood aside. With a dramatic flourish he removed the cover and revealed the most astounding piece of furniture his guests had ever seen.

"Allow me to present my exquisite 'Siege d'Amour', or in plain English, my 'Seat of Love'!" The assembled partygoers stood and gazed in silent wonder at the strange contraption.

"In front of you," announced their host, "is a faithful reproduction of my original, which now stands proudly in my favourite Parisian bordello, Le Chabanais – a shrine to pleasure, and very familiar to the gentlemen amongst us." This was greeted by a general outburst of laughter and applause.

"You wonder at it," he continued, "and well you may. This little device of mine is able to accommodate up to four lovers at a time. A variety of interesting positions may be obtained, half the fun is working out how!" This comment prompted much jollity from his admirers.

"I decided some time ago that this little invention, which has afforded me so much pleasure, needs to be shared. So I had another re-created for the delectation of you – my dear friends." This announcement was met with cheers all round.

"I am no longer as athletic as I would like to be, but nevertheless, this exquisite construction more than compensates for that!" The visitors were now exuberant.

"The time has come to christen her! Are there any volunteers who would like to commence with the proceedings?"

The revellers now fuelled by champagne and other substances, were now in various states of nakedness and excitement, so little encouragement was required. A general clamour now took place among the more adventurous hedonists, as several portly gentlemen and their partners hurled themselves upon the contraption. An almighty struggle took place as they attempted to avail themselves of an advantageous position. There was a mad thrashing of naked arms, legs and not to mention derrières. A loud groaning noise and a resounding crash followed, as 'The

Siege d'Amour' gave way under the weight of all the writhing pleasure-seekers, and as it disintegrated, its occupants were tumbled onto the floor in an ungainly heap. Hurrahs, cheers and laughter erupted from the drunken spectators, who had decided that a spot of voyeurism would afford the best entertainment. Bertie was not at all amused at this spectacle and flew into an apoplectic rage, striding among his fallen guests, cursing and admonishing them for their ridiculous and undignified behaviour. He shouted and continued to walk in circles around the heap of naked bodies, ranting as he went.

"So, this is how you repay my hospitality. Yes, you Lord Chancellor. It's no good cowering behind the Archbishop there." None of the shame-faced offenders was spared their host's anger. No less than three of his favourite mistresses attempted to disengage themselves from the sprawling mass of naked dignitaries and shamefacedly offered their apologies for their rash and boisterous behaviour.

Eventually, his tirade ceased and he threw himself upon a sofa, toying with his buttonhole, his Royal pride hurt by the callous behaviour of his guests. He was followed by his troupe of 'lovelies' who fussed over him with kisses, whispers, tickles and pinches. Slowly, his annoyance subsided and within minutes his mood had mellowed enough for him to raise a half-hearted smile and to invite his guests to recommence with their debaucheries. Then he ordered his flunkies to remove the wreckage from his sight. At that, 'the man in black' stepped forward and addressed his superior.

"Sir, I cannot offer to replace your wondrous seat of love, but I have now obtained something for which you have long desired." The man clicked his fingers and several assistants stepped forward with the open coffin, which they placed at Bertie's feet. Peering in at the contents of the casket greedily, he stroked his beard, drew heavily on his cigar, exhaled a thick cloud of smoke, coughed, gulped more champagne and exclaimed, "Splendid, truly splendid. Good Lord, some of these cod pieces are magnificent, enough to make your eyes water though, not to mention the Memsahibs, what, what!" This remark caused some of the ladies to shriek with laughter.

"What a splendid collection, well... I find myself almost speechless." He stooped down with some difficulty, opening a snuffbox, and stared at the contents. Upon a black velvet pad there huddled a small clump of bright red crinkly hairs under which was a small inscription which read: 'Plucked from Nell Gwynne by Sir Garfield Numbshaft, protector of his Majesty King Charles II's Royal Pubic Hair Collection'. He then carefully removed one of the ginger follicles between his finger and thumb, placed it under his nose and sniffed.

"Hmmm... not bad, considering its age." And he replaced the sample lovingly.

"These wonderful historic exhibits will afford me hours and hours of amusement. My thanks to those responsible for a job well done."

"Please, Sir," replied 'the man in black'. "May I beg your indulgence by introducing you to the people who, shall we say, 'acquired' these items for you." He gestured for the three miscreants to step forward. They bowed and curtsied self consciously, aware that they were the only fully dressed members of the party apart from, of course, the staff.

"May I introduce Lord Methane and his wife Lady Bulimia Puke," 'the man in black' presented.

"And this, gentleman, is her twin brother, Professor Biryani."

Chapter 11

Corruption, deceit and betrayal

As Bertie offered his hand in welcome and appreciation, Gridlock signalled behind to Todger and Prunestone that he'd heard enough, and they crawled out from their hiding places. The inspector blew his whistle, and the other policemen appeared in an instant and surrounded the assembled gathering. As they did so, the partygoers attempted to cover their 'privates' while standing in silence and bewilderment.

"Who the hell are you?" exploded the 'Caresser'. "How dare you enter this place uninvited!" The naked guests and clothed attendants had now crowded together in an attempt to threaten. Unperturbed, Gridlock addressed the host with grim conviction.

"May it please you sir, that standing before you are three of the most ruthless and notorious villains this country has ever had the misfortune to produce. We have been on their trail for some time, and it now seems clear that these treasures were stolen to order, by these three villains. I dread to think how our beloved Queen would feel if she knew that these robberies had been instigated in order to adorn this den of iniquity." Becoming even more authoritative, he pointed his finger at the accused.

"Unless these items are returned to their rightful place immediately and these criminals put behind bars, I shall have no hesitation in making what I have witnessed, known to the public and to the proper authorities. Scotland Yard's Inspector Todger here will bear witness to the perversions we have had the misfortune to observe." At this point Gridlock glanced at Todger for reassurance and support.

"Now, steady on Gridlock old boy," muttered the inspector, coughing nervously. "I need to think about this," he said and glimpsed from the corner of his eye, his superior, the Chief Commissioner of Police who was standing awkwardly, attempting to cover his nudity in the crowd.

"Evenin' sir!" Todger saluted uncomfortably and continued, "Now don't lets be so hasty my friend, these people here appear to be just indulging in some harmless fun, and I'm sure that these items here were just borrowed for the evenin' as part of a jolly jape. Please forgive my colleague Gridlock Spumes, sir, for he has not considered the gravity of the accusations that he has made. I'm sure that this matter can be sorted out with the utmost discretion."

Phuckwytte then stepped forward, curtsied awkwardly and blubbered, "Oh, yes, yes indeed sir. May I beg for your indulgence, as I apologise profusely for intruding upon what is obviously a private jollification. As far as I'm aware, I know nothing and haven't seen anything untoward," he lied.

"Silence, you cowards! Am I being betrayed?" Gridlock barked angrily. "These monsters who have committed these crimes must be brought to justice! You know that, as well as I do! What the hell's the matter with you two?" Gridlock demanded. "Speak out, in God's name, speak out!"

"Dear, dear, Mr Spumes," chuckled Bertie. "You really are getting yourself into a state aren't you. Please understand that your threats are quite pointless… isn't that so Chief Justice?"

"Quite pointless," a voice answered from the crowd.

"And what do you say Home Secretary?"

"Agreed," returned another voice.

Turning to Inspector Todger, he recommended, "Your loyalty and vow of secrecy which I know you will make, shall not go unrewarded, for I intend to make you a Knight of the Realm and your new appointment of promotion will of course be met with a substantial increase in salary. Please be so good as to kneel. Alas, I have no sword available – something else will have to suffice." One of his ladies in attendance giggled and handed him a curious looking object from one of the South Pacific Islands that had been designed for use during fertility ceremonies. Its handle was of wood and leather, decorated with shark's teeth and sea shells. A coconut bedecked with colourful feathers, adorned the other end. The host looked at it, smiled and laid it upon each of Todger's shoulders in turn.

"Rise now, sir… Err… Whom am I addressing?"

"Todger, your Royal Highness."

"Very well, arise Sir Todger, Chief Superintendent." The inspector knelt, bowed his head and raised himself, stepping back proudly.

"And you sir. Who are you pray?" he enquired addressing the doctor.

"Doctor Phuckwytte Prunestone, sir, at your service," came the reply.

"So it would seem!" chuckled the Caresser.

"Now, what are we to do with you?" He eyed the cross-dresser up and down thoughtfully. "Hmmm... Yes I have it! We will make you Master of Ceremonies... or is it Mistress?" he joked.

"Here in our little 'Palace of Pleasure'. It would be a position of great importance that would enable you to socialise in the highest of circles. As you can see, we have no prejudices here, in fact we have several gentlemen who, like yourself are a little light on their feet and who bat for the other side, so to speak. Isn't that right Mr Wilde? I am sure they would find your little affectations quite delectable! So what do you say?" Blushing, the doctor stepped forward bowed and began to mumble incoherently with joy at the prospect of what he considered to be a grand position.

"Such an honour, Your Highness, such a honour," he beamed. "You can rely on me to carry out my duties diligently and with the utmost secrecy." He curtsied, bowed and stepped back on the hem of his ripped dress and stumbled backwards into the open coffin. As he struggled to regain his composure, a particularly ornate cod piece was now set firmly at a fairly rakish angle upon his head, which gave him the appearance of a Court Jester, much to the delight of the crowd. Uncontrolled hilarity erupted at the spectacle to which Bertie joined in, and soon, floods of tears began to roll down his fat face. He then pulled Phuckwytte out of his predicament, shook his hand and patted him on the shoulder, suggesting that when the doctor commenced his duties, it might be appropriate for him to shave off his sideburns, and handlebar moustache, since these could be considered a blemish upon his femininity.

At this point in the proceedings, Gridlock stood quivering with rage and cried out, "Enough of this charade." He then crammed allsorts into his mouth, and eyed the doctor and the inspector contemptuously. "You may think you've triumphed over me," he shouted almost inaudibly, spraying liquorice everywhere. "The silence and loyalty of these two so-called men may be bought at the right price! But you will not silence Gridlock Spumes! I sir, am a man of honour!" His sentence was cut short by a well aimed kick on his rear-end by Lady Bulimia Puke as her brother emptied a bottle of champagne over him. Gridlock rose to his full height, wiped his face on his sleeve and drew his pistol.

"Mock me if you will, but I would rather languish in Newgate Prison and be branded a traitor, than bend to your vile demands."

"Come now, detective Gridlock," confided the fat host. "I have been informed on good authority that your successful exploits are known throughout the length of the land, to the extent that your name has become a household word. I can't quite remember what it is at the moment, but nevertheless what I'm trying to say is that the government is in desperate need of someone of your calibre to fill the post of Commander in Chief of our Intelligence Service. A tempting prospect, what do you say? Of course a seat in the House of Lords could go with it and a little country estate perhaps?"

"Never!" Gridlock shouted, completely losing control. "I'd rather be imprisoned for life!" he screamed.

"Then that is precisely what you will be," considered Bertie. "Seize him and take him away!" he ordered and with that, his personal guards wrestled the detective's weapon from him and tied his hands together. One of the female guests offered her camiknickers that were unceremoniously pulled over the unfortunate detective's head, as he was dragged from the chamber.

Phuckwytte escorted him out and apologised. "Forgive me Gridlock, but I'm only acting for the best."

"Acting for your best, you mean, and poor acting at that. You traitor!" came the muffled reply. Gridlock was bundled towards the exit, bellowing, "I, Gridlock Spumes will make sure that you will all pay the price for your evil deeds no matter who you are or how powerful. I promise you!" The sound of his tirade echoed around the tunnel and gradually faded into the distance. Meanwhile the 'Caresser' continued to address his guests.

"Pray, continue with our little celebration my friends, do not let this trifling interruption spoil our fun and games. Champagne for everyone!" And with that, the orchestra struck up a rendition of 'The military two-step'. Phuckwytte, on hearing the music could not resist giving the partygoers a full demonstration of his dubious dancing technique, whilst his sightless master was led back up the huge stairway, returning to street level, still hooded with his hands tied behind his back.

The sounds and smells of the Thames were unmistakable to him as he was pushed down into some kind of small boat, which his captors began to row in silence.

After a considerable length of time, a man's booming voice ordered them to, "Heave too an' come aside." With help on each side he was forced to alight back onto terra firma. They then stepped over what he imagined to be a hawser or chain, and then down a steep and narrow companionway. He was untied and his blindfold was removed to reveal a large room with a low ceiling, lit by a single oil lamp.

"Give me just a few moments with him," requested Todger to the man in charge.

"Very well, but don't be too long. We're expected back within the hour and you will find out to your cost that the Prince does not like to be kept waiting." And with that, the ruffian climbed up the wooden steps and joined the others outside.

The inspector now approached the detective cautiously. "Gridlock old man, I had no idea that things would go this far, believe me. You must realise that I have no jurisdiction whatsoever over these men, as they are not the police. And apart from that, nobody's sorrier about this business than I am. But you can see what a spot I'm in."

"Call yourself 'the law'… What law? Your own bloody law! You have been bought like a common whore," was the prisoner's terse reply.

"Now look here, I can't just go arresting half the dignitaries in London. Some of them are my direct superiors, for God's sake!

In my position I have got to play the game, keep my mouth shut and do as I'm told. Don't you see old man, if you swear to secrecy like I did, I'll put a good word in for you, and you'll be out of here in no time." Gridlock was not listening and in no mood to be persuaded.

"You and that half-wit Prunestone, I cannot believe what you have done or how you'll be able to sleep at night after this outrageous denial of justice!" Todger ignored this criticism and tried to pacify him.

"Look. I appreciate how you must feel, but if there's anything I can get for you; liquorice, tobacco or even your violin – just say the word and old Todger will see you get it."

"Sir Todger, don't you mean?" replied Gridlock disdainfully. "There is nothing more I want from you, since you have already sold your soul to the highest bidder. Now please remove yourself at once and leave me alone." The inspector doffed his hat uncomfortably, bid farewell and climbed the steps, making his exit through the hatchway, which was slammed shut and bolted behind him.

Gridlock now surveyed the damp and decaying surroundings in which he was incarcerated, and as he was doing so, he felt a moving sensation under his feet. It was now clear that he was not on land as he had previously thought, but still upon the water and in the hold of a much larger vessel, possibly a Thames sailing barge. The remains of past cargos of hay, grain and sand that littered the floor substantiated the fact, but at present the space was filled with large coils of hemp rope. On the walls were messages and graffiti, some carved, some written in candle smoke, and perhaps even blood or worse. The place had obviously been used to house prisoners for some considerable time. The area remaining was sparse, containing a small three-legged stool, a china chamber pot, and in one corner there were some old sacks filled with straw, which served as a bed. A table was placed against the stern wall on which there was a chipped enamel mug and jug along with a few old books, which were covered in mildew. Gridlock took the lamp over to peruse their contents and by its flickering light blew the dust from them and read their covers: *How to knit your own furniture* by Nugent Quilt was one title. Another read, *Home dentistry for beginners* by Dr Vanden Rindmold, and yet another, *A hundred and one ways to cook rhubarb* by Miss Dolores Throat. He then began to read the messages from past prisoners that covered the timbered walls. One read: 'Twenty glorious years away from the wife! Maurice Anthrax, 1822'. Another, 'A life on the ocean waves! Warrington Minge, Actor. March 1846' and yet another unsigned 'God forgive me and release me from the wretched hole!'

"Hmmm," wondered Gridlock, "I wonder why he ended up here, dereliction of duty perhaps." The next was a rude drawing under which a little rhyme had been scrawled: 'Wherever ye be let thy wynde blow free for keeping it in t'was the death of me! Sir Titus Scroat, 1814'. These sad messages of past prisoners went on and on.

I wonder how many innocent wretches have been tortured and hurled down into this miserable prison? Gridlock thought to himself. Now in a state of sheer exhaustion, hungry, miserable and in the depths of despair, having spent the whole night trying to make sense of his predicament, he laid on the floor, having rolled up the camiknickers into a pillow, and wondered who their owner might be, and as the lamp began to die, he lost all reason to exist. Finally he was woken by the sound of tuneless singing from above and when the hatch was opened, brilliant sunlight flooded in and blinded him. His gaoler was an old 'sea dog' of a man, with a weathered complexion. He sported a gold tooth, (his only one) and an earring to match. What little hair remained on top of his head was pulled back tightly to form a small pigtail at the back. Dressed in rough bargeman's clothes, he walked like most seafaring folk, with a rolling gait, which he rolled frequently.

"I've brought 'e some vitals shipmate," he announced as he climbed down into the hold and handed Gridlock a bowl of steaming fish head soup.

"Thank you," said the famished detective and after forcing down several mouthfuls, he introduced himself.

"Gridlock Spumes, Private Detective," he said, while spitting out a mouthful of fish bones. The man held out a gnarled hand.

"Erasmus Whelk, skipper of 'The Gay Barnacle'," and they shook hands. At that moment a scruffy pimple-ridden head appeared through the hatchway that prompted Whelk to explain.

"My son, Eli," he announced. "Chief cook an' bottle washer." Gridlock nodded in recognition at the innocent lad, whose topsail in his opinion, didn't appear to reach the full mast.

"I really do need to get back home to Baker Street," said the detective. "It's a matter of great urgency!"

"You'll 'ave a long swim then, shipmate," chortled Captain Whelk, "We're three mile off 'Arwich."

"What! Where the hell are you bound for?"

"Lowestoft," came the reply. "Bonne appetite!" And with that, he continued to sing as he climbed the creaking steps.

"Come get yer duds in order. For we's goin' t' leave tomorra. 'Eave away, me jollies, 'eave away," and he slammed the hatch door shut. Eventually, during the following day, Gridlock was allowed to 'take a turn' around the deck and to empty his chamber pot over the side. He gazed out to sea and realised that escape was impossible. It would be suicide to try and swim the three miles ashore as the current was so powerful. Death would surely ensue by drowning, due to physical exhaustion. His evenings were passed in complete isolation, having to endure his captors' drunken tuneless disharmony, as they murdered sea-shanties in their cabin next door. During these interludes he reflected on the course of events that had led him to his present miserable predicament. As their destination was reached he was strapped to the anchor winch while the ship's consignment was unloaded. Hours later as the operation was completed, he was taken below and imprisoned yet again. The captain then set sail back along the east coast calling in at Southwold to take on his own personal provisions of tobacco and rum. From Ipswich they took on ninety tons of grain to keep Gridlock company for the rest of the voyage. This cargo caused him to have chronic bouts of hay fever. Their final call was to take on a few dozen barrels of salted meat at Burnham-on-Crouch.

After several days of enduring monotonous and mind-numbing confinement, the hatch was opened early one morning, and a whimpering, ragged, and hooded wretch was thrown into the hold.

"And who might you be?" he asked and then recognised the intruder.

"Phuckwytte!" he exclaimed. "You Idiot! You Judas! If any little shit deserves to be shut up here, it's you!"

"Oh Gridlock!" the moustache-less Phuckwytte pleaded, now on his knees. "Don't you, Oh Gridlock me, you betrayed me, you turncoat!"

"I couldn't help it," the doctor cried and began his usual jabbering of excuses.

"But why the devil have they brought you here? Speak man, out with it!"

"Oh, forgive me, please forgive me Gridlock, I've been such a fool. You don't know the suffering I've had to endure, for I discovered too late how base and treacherous these people are." With that he began to sob uncontrollably, saving his controlled sobs for the weekends including bank holidays. It was then that Gridlock (while scratching his backside) felt a slight sympathetic twinge of remorse,* prompting him to lay his other hand gently upon the doctor's shoulder to comfort him.

"Pray continue." Regaining his composure the doctor went on to explain.

---

*If you, by some unexplainable reason, also feel a sight sympathetic twinge of remorse reading this, we recommend you consult your Physician.

"They treated me abominably, all their promises were broken and I was forced to become... well, how can I put it... to be a...a... lavatory attendant!"

"By Royal appointment, I've no doubt!" smirked Gridlock. At this remark Phuckwytte broke down again.

"That is how I spent my days, cleaning the bowls, mopping the floor and polishing the brass fittings."

"Dreadful," remarked his master sarcastically.

"But whenever they held one of their disgusting soirees, I was released, dressed up as a common music hall tart and commanded to perform all kinds of lewd songs and dances for their amusement."

"No change there then," said Gridlock as his manservant continued.

"Gentlemen of a certain persuasion tried to take advantage of me, but willpower and my reinforced industrial strength canvas drawers deterred them, thank God. In desperation when I could stand their brutish treatment no longer, I told them that unless they released me immediately, I would eventually escape and make known everything I had endured to the newspapers. This was greeted by the usual jeering taunts and laughter."

"Hmmm, I see," said the detective unimpressed at the thought of Phuckwytte's dilemma.

"But why have they put us in here?" Phuckwytte enquired.

"Well, my guess is, that at the moment, not only are we out of the way, but we are also untraceable. In a real prison everything has to be done by the book. They would have a record of our whereabouts, by whom we were arrested, for what, where and when."

"Oh I see," his new cellmate admitted. "Am I forgiven, Gridlock?"

"Well... I suppose so," came the reluctant reply.

"You've always been a rash and impetuous little... How can I put it?"

"Buffoon?" offered Phuckwytte.

"No, cretin," his master corrected. "However, we must find a way out of this place. Now there are two of us we might possibly stand a chance." Gridlock, despite his misgivings, was now secretly pleased to have some company. Now, as their captors continued their drunken singing, he began to formulate a possible means of escape.

Chapter 12

Escape to freedom

At anchor one evening, Gridlock discovered an old discarded candle and on lighting it found a rat hole in the timber wall, between the skipper's cabin next door and their own prison in the hold. Lying on the floor under the table he was able to eavesdrop on what little conversation was taking place. "What on earth are you doing down there?" Phuckwytte asked, thinking that the isolation had finally got to his employer.

"I'm listening," answered Gridlock.

"Jesus, what the hell for? Their singing's bloody awful!" complained the doctor. After what seemed nearly an hour of drunken performance, at last their captors' conversation turned to discussing the 'Gay Barnacle's' next trip. It appeared that as there were now two prisoners to feed, they would have to work their passage by helping to load the next cargo. This unwelcome information put Phuckwytte on his usual defence.

"I'm not a bloody labourer!" he announced. "And I'm certainly not cut out for heavy-duty man's work."

"We've got no choice," explained Gridlock. "We've got to eat."

"I'd rather starve," Phuckwytte moaned.

"Don't be silly, we need our strength to escape. We'll have to bide our time and wait for the first opportunity that presents itself."

The following morning, the trip upriver was to collect building rubble from a site that was being redeveloped. They joined the gang of quayside workers and sweated blood on their first day and many days after, shovelling rubble into barrows and tipping the contents into the hold. The shock of this backbreaking labour was overwhelming and it took its toll, reducing our heroes to grovelling wrecks after a few hours. 'The Gay Barnacle' would be their 'home' for the next few months, navigating up and down the river and with occasional trips around the coast. As time passed the weather became warmer and with spring arriving, their cargo now changed to cattle cake, sugar and rubber, all of which was easier to load. Gradually, Captain Whelk began to trust them a little more and he relaxed his grip by giving them a certain amount of freedom. Sometimes if they were lucky they would barter extra food in exchange for stolen goods when the odd crate was 'accidentally' damaged and opened. It was during one of these occasions whilst going upriver that their fortunes were to change in their favour. This was Phuckwytte's old stamping ground and he was still remembered by some of his old friends and acquaintances, despite the fact that he now resembled an Irish navvy, without the physical attributes.

One morning he was recognised by one of his old 'chums', a 'River man' by the name of Sid Goitre, who made his living by rifling the pockets of floating corpses in the river, a common occurrence during this period. It was he and a couple of his drinking cronies who, after hearing of Phuckwytte's sad plight decided to help, and soon a plan of escape was formulated. If it were to succeed, a neap tide along with some kind of distraction or diversion would help to make it work. One evening, while bales of wool were being loaded onto the barge, one of Sid's men set light to a bale stack on the quay, which caused chaos. In the panic that ensued, our two prisoners meanwhile hid under a tarpaulin in Sid's flat-bottomed boat. They were then transported up-river, to the lower end of St Saviour's Dock, a small creek in Bermondsey's Upper Pool; from there they would make good their escape. After thanking Sid and his helpers, they strove inland in the driving rain, searching for some form of transport to get them home.

"Ah, free at last!" gasped Gridlock. And with that they attempted to hail a hansom cab, but to no avail, for every time a cabbie glanced at the filthy and unkempt pair, they cracked their whips and were off again.

"Nothing for it, we'll have to walk or try and scrounge a lift," remarked Gridlock as they cut across towards Borough Market, unaware that they were being followed. Although they resembled a pair of homeless vagrants they still managed to hitch lifts from kind-hearted travellers, who took pity, and made room for them on their vehicle. Their first successful ride was on a removal wagon, which was returning to its depot; the second was on an ice cart; and the last ultimate sensation, was on a horseless carriage which was being delivered to its new owner in Hampstead. They were now at last in their home territory of Baker Street. It was late and not wishing to disturb their housekeeper, Lilly, at such a late hour, they decided to come in the rear tradesmen's entrance, obtaining a hidden door key under a fat gaudy garden gnome, (that had been purchased on a previous holiday to Germany) the secret entry that Gridlock had used previously.

Within minutes they had washed, changed and were seated in their favourite armchairs.

"Home at last!" said Phuckwytte trying to encourage the miserable excuse for a fire that was now nearly out. He then threw on some more damp coal which extinguished it all together.

"Time now for a stiff drink, old bean," suggested Gridlock as he went to the drinks cabinet and poured them both a large measure of dandelion and burdock.

"Bottoms up!" he toasted.

"Cheers," Phuckwytte responded. They sat for some time in silence as they sipped their cordial. At last Phuckwytte enquired, "What now then old boy?"

"We must make haste to Buckingham Palace," was the immediate reply.

"Buckingham Palace?" repeated the doctor.

"Yes, to Buckingham Palace where we must seek an audience with our beloved Queen."

"Queen?"

"Yes, Queen," snapped the detective. "What are you, a bloody parrot? It is imperative that a private meeting with Her Majesty be arranged, for she must be informed of the shocking events which we have uncovered."

"But…but…" stumbled Phuckwytte. "We can't possibly; it will break the old girl's heart. She's miserable enough as it is. Is there no other way?" he asked.

"None," was the stern reply. "It's our duty Prunestone, not only to her, but also to the country." Gridlock now stood statesmanlike and gazed out of the window and continued, "I'm afraid that as a result, heads will roll, the government may fall, our church and legal system could be in danger and the whole fabric of our society could break down. So you see, my dear Phuckwytte, the fate of 'Old Blighty' would seem to be resting on our shoulders at this very minute. If we say and do nothing, then the country could remain under a cloud of corruption, greed and decadence. But on the other hand…" (at this point there was almost an insane intensity in his patchless eye).

"With our help, the moral fibre of our great Empire will remain intact." This patriotic claptrap was interrupted by the apparition of a toothless Lilly. She appeared in the doorway dressed in a moth-eaten nightgown, and cap – a shocking sight to behold.

"I 'eard voices," she complained. At that moment, the tinkle of the front door bell rang in the hall downstairs.

"Who the hell can that be at this hour? Go and see to it Lilly," he ordered. In a few moments, he heard her puffing up the stairs as she returned, clutching a brown paper parcel.

"This 'ere's for you Mr Spumes, some toff brung it to the door. A tall gent in evenin' dress, posh voice, said I was to give it to yer, personal like."

"Bring it here woman," ordered Gridlock officiously.

"Ooohh, listen to that. Wot did yer last servant die of?" She gave the package to her employer, turned, swivelled on her false leg and hobbled away, slamming the door behind her.

"Hmmm," the detective pondered as he put the parcel on the table. "Get me the scissors from the desk, old boy." He carefully cut the string and tore open the paper that wrapped an old shoebox. Attached to the lid was a birthday card that read: 'Happy Birthday Gridlock'.

"Strange, it's not my birthday!" he mused. Inside the greeting read: 'Goodbye Mr Spumes'.

Funny, I'm not going anywhere, he thought. "Hmmm... curious, it's not signed." Removing the lid of the box he took out a brass alarm clock. "Nice of whomever it is to send me a timepiece. It's just what I wanted." He shook it and held it to his ear. "Seems to be going all right. What do you think of it?" handing it to Phuckwytte.

"Well now..." was the hesitant reply. "In my opinion it looks very much like... well I hate to say this... but..." Now the two men stared at each other in frozen terror for a couple of seconds, until, in unison they both screamed:

"It looks like a a... b...bloody B..B...Bomb!"

Phuckwytte ran to the door, opened it to find their ancient housekeeper bent over with her ear to the keyhole in her usual eavesdropping position. He thrust the bomb into her hands and demanded that she should throw it out of the front window into the street.

"Bloody 'ell, I don't know, I'm nothin' but a bleedin' servant round here," she mumbled.

"You are a bleedin' servant round here!" reminded Gridlock as she made her way to the front parlour and called back, "Nice clock like this one, bit fussy ain'cha, what's up wiv't it?" Just then the alarm went off just as she ejected it out of the window, resulting in a blinding flash and an almighty explosion. Poor Lilly (her drawers in tatters) was blown back through the doorway into the arms of Phuckwytte, both of them landing in a dusty heap.

The detective however remained calmly seated, brushed some debris from his shoulder and lap, sipped his dust-polluted drink, puffed on his pipe and replied, "If I'm not very much mistaken Prunestone, it seems that in all likelihood that bomb was intended for us and we could still be in grave danger."

Gridlock put down his glass, went over and extracted his housekeeper from beneath Phuckwytte, painstakingly picking her up and after a few moments brought her round with smelling salts and a nip of brandy. After she'd recovered a little, they then picked their way through the remains of the front window that littered the floor and descended the stairs to the pavement, where amongst other debris caused by the explosion they found Lilly's wooden leg that appeared to have knocked out a passing pedestrian. As they stepped over the unconscious gentleman they realised that it was none other than Methane Puke.

"Hmmm…there's rough justice for you!" smiled the detective. A constable had already been summoned to the scene of the explosion and Gridlock ordered him to arrest the unconscious man without delay. They then pushed their way through the crowd that had formed, and stepping into the road, hailed a cab.

"To Buckingham Palace," cried the detective. "And then onwards to justice and freedom, to victory and honour!"

"Righty-ho guv," replied the cabbie, "to Buckin'am Palace and then on to the 'Justice an' Freedom' and the 'Victory an' Honour', 'ere, hang about, I knows all the boozers round 'ere, but I've never 'eard o' them two. You'll 'ave to give me directions."

Could this be the end, or just the beginning?

The Gridlock Spumes

'Power of Detection Test'

Can you put a name to some of the characters displayed here in our specially-compiled portrait gallery? Endless fun can be obtained by those stoic readers who have managed to wade through our story and who find themselves with even more time to waste.

Some of the more accomplished amateur sleuths will of course be able to supply the correct name to each of the characters by simply using their powers of memory and intuition.

The more mentally-challenged will no doubt find themselves flicking backwards and forwards between the pages until they have completed the conundrum successfully.

The very best of luck to you all.